Three Minutes a Day

VOLUME 43

Other Christopher Books in Print

Father James Keller's
You Can Change the World
Anniversary Edition

and other volumes in the
Three Minutes a Day
series

THREE MINUTES A DAY
VOLUME 43

Mary Ellen Robinson
Vice President, The Christophers

Stephanie Raha
Editor-in-Chief

Margaret O'Connell
Senior Research Editor

Contributors
Joan Bromfield
Karen Hazel Radenbaugh
Monica Ann Yehle-Glick

Contributing Interns
Kimberly Colon
Kenneth Frank
Rebecca Kelleher
Mary Beth Mullarkey
Jennifer Nelson
Maria Puig

The Christophers
5 Hanover Square, 11th Floor
New York, NY 10004

I lift my eyes to the hills —
from where will my help come?
My help comes from the Lord,
who made heaven and earth.

He will not let your foot be moved;
He who keeps you will not slumber.
He who keeps Israel
will neither slumber nor sleep.

The Lord is your keeper;
the Lord is your shade at your right hand.
The sun shall not strike you by day,
nor the moon by night.

The Lord will keep you from all evil;
He will keep your life.
The Lord will keep your going out and your coming in
from this time on and forevermore.

PSALM 121

Introduction

What do you want to get out of your day?

Many people might say something like, "I just want to do my job without too many hassles. Run my errands and spend some time with family and friends." And that's fine—as far as it goes.

Most of us want something more. We want to know that our lives have meaning. We want our work and our relationships, all we have and do and are, to create a life of meaning for ourselves and the world around us.

Father James Keller, who founded The Christophers, said: "Greatness of outlook and purpose can inspire anyone to contribute to the common good. But more and more individuals are beginning to realize that without the major ingredient of divine motivation they will never experience true fulfillment or satisfaction."

Within the pages of this new edition of *Three Minutes a Day*, we hope you'll find encouragement to meet your daily responsibilities and inspiration to welcome God's loving presence—not only for three minutes a day, but for the other 1,437 as well.

Jerry Costello and
Mary Ellen Robinson
for The Christophers

Are You Resolved?

What's your News Year's resolution?

Many people make resolutions to better their lives at the start of each year. Popular ones include efforts to lose weight; to quit a bad habit, such as smoking; or to improve personal finances.

Some people concentrate on spiritual growth by resolving to read the Bible regularly or to spend more time in prayer.

Here are two other worthwhile ideas from 18th-century American theologian and philosopher Jonathan Edwards: "I resolve not only to refrain from an air of dislike, fretfulness, and anger in conversation, but to exhibit an air of love, cheerfulness and gentleness. ...I resolve never to do any manner of thing, whether in soul or body, except what tends to the glory of God."

Resolutions are hard to fulfill. If they were easy, we wouldn't need to make such a strong decision in the first place. But, if we persevere, they can truly transform us.

Be persistent. (2 Timothy 4:2)

Eternal Father, guide my efforts to be more and more the person You made me to be.

Major Career Shift

Career changers often want to use their skills and interests to help others as well as themselves.

During her divorce, Theresa Wilson's career shift began with a home-made blessing basket containing friends' supportive cards and letters. When she mentioned this blessing basket during public-speaking engagements, listeners wanted their own.

Wilson decided to help. Today the Blessing Basket Project is improving the lives of weavers in Ghana, Uganda, Indonesia, Bangladesh and Papua, New Guinea. They are paid as much as $12 for every three baskets they weave.

With that money, women can buy nutritious food for their children; pay for textbooks and school uniforms. A Ugandan woman even gained the financial freedom to leave her abusive husband, send her four sons to school, and open a restaurant.

It's never too late to make a positive difference.

Faith by itself, if it has no works, is dead. (James 2:17)

Guide me, Spirit of Wisdom, in choosing a career that will help me grow and change lives.

Reliving Childhood

Although experience brings wisdom, people sometimes leave important things behind as they mature. The peace and fun of childhood need not end as adulthood begins. Consider these suggestions from Dr. Judith Orloff:

- Explore your background.
- Be active. It enhances productivity, reduces blood pressure, and builds a stronger immune system.
- Look at the world and be amazed.
- Choose adventure.
- Think "different." Unfamiliar decisions keep you agile.
- Live in the moment.
- Lower your guard.
- Remember the things that make you smile.
- Banish "I must" and have fun.

And talk to the experts: children can be your best teachers.

Unless you change and become like children, you will never enter the kingdom of heaven. (Matthew 18:3)

Lord of life, keep my spirit young.

The Gift of Gratitude

Do you appreciate all your blessings? Or do you find yourself focusing more on what you don't have and what's wrong with your life? When was the last time you really felt grateful to God and, yes, His children?

Melodie Beattie, the author of several books including *Codependent No More* and *Language of Letting Go,* has this to say about the subject:

"Gratitude unlocks the fullness of life. It turns what we have into enough, and more. It turns denial into acceptance, chaos into order, confusion into clarity. ...It turns problems into gifts, failures into success, the unexpected into perfect timing, and mistakes into important events. Gratitude makes sense of our past, brings peace for today and creates a vision for tomorrow."

Make "thank you" part of your life—not just every day, but every hour.

Be thankful. ...and with gratitude in your hearts sing...to God. And whatever you do in word or deed, do everything in the name of the Lord Jesus, giving thanks to God the Father through Him. (Colossians 15,16-17)

Thank You, Savior, for all You give me, but above all, for the gift of Yourself.

Keep the Change

Saving spare change in a jar for a rainy day is nothing new. Recently, however, the practice has gained approval among financiers. Financial planning expert Suze Orman recommends that people save spare change and invest the coins in the stock market.

Richard Bauman and his wife, Donna, followed this advice and saved their spare change—to the tune of over $400 a year—but took a different approach when it came to investing it. Rather than invest in stocks, they chose to support programs that help others "have a better life," they say.

They donated to an organization that feeds the hungry, one that provides decent housing to the needy, and another that trains individuals to become self-sufficient.

How can your simple efforts improve the lives of others? Like the Baumans, a relatively simple task—like putting a few coins in a jar—can positively affect another's life.

How ample a little is for a well-disciplined person! (Sirach 31:19)

Remind me that great change begins with one small step, Lord God.

Serving a Portion of Love with the Soup

In a sense, running a soup kitchen and serving food are the easy parts. It's the spirit with which you serve that's important.

Joe's Soup Kitchen in Langley, British Columbia, Canada, sounds like a warm and welcoming place. A "lot of love" goes into the soup according to founder Joyce Waldbillig.

Together with volunteers, she regularly cooks and serves gallons of hearty soups so people "go away feeling full"—full of unconditional love and soup.

One homeless guest spoke for many when he said that the volunteers are very caring people. Waldbillig adds that "if someone doesn't come in for a week or two, I worry about them. Top priority is respect. We're not here to judge."

Not judging; nourishing with love and good nutrition—these make people, homeless or not, thrive.

Come you that are blessed by My Father...for I was hungry and you gave me food...thirsty and you gave me...drink...a stranger and you welcomed me. (Matthew 25:34,35)

Remind us, Jesus, that when we volunteer at a soup kitchen or shelter we are volunteering to serve You.

Rockin' With the Lord

The Rev. Dr. Paige Blair of St. George's Episcopal Church in York, Maine, didn't think her decision to play rock music during liturgies was revolutionary. She simply wanted "spiritually rich and social-justice oriented" music to reinforce the messages of her ministry. Yet, when the British media caught wind of her flair for rock, the event was broadcasted on the BBC, among other mainstream media outlets.

Rev. Dr. Blair relies heavily on the music of Irish rock group U2, which has demonstrated its commitment to AIDS awareness and social justice in recent years. Blair says U2's music, which has long been recognized for its Christian themes, lends itself to religious services. "They [U2] have always been open about their spirituality," says Blair, commenting that many of the group's lyrics come straight from Scripture.

God, spirituality, and concern for social justice can be found in every musical style. Leading by example is one way to teach others to see God everywhere.

Praise God in His sanctuary...with trumpet...lute and harp! Praise Him with tambourine and dance...with strings and pipe!...Praise the Lord! (Psalm 150:1,3-4,6)

Holy Spirit, bless Your people with wise and courageous clergy.

The Story Behind the Story Board

Anyone who has seen the cartoon *Scooby Doo* knows it's a zany, wacky cartoon about a gang of curious, but well-meaning, teens and their dog, who are determined to solve mysteries and put bad guys behind bars.

The silliness of the cartoon, however, belies the artist who created the mystery-loving Great Dane. Iwao Takamoto learned his craft in a Japanese-American internment camp. On his release, he lugged notebooks full of hand-drawn sketches to the major Hollywood movie studios, looking for work.

His unique style and persistence caught the interest of executives at Walt Disney Studios, who hired him to work on animated films such as *Lady and the Tramp* and *101 Dalmatians*. Eventually, he had a prolific 40-year career at Hanna-Barbera studios, where he created the crime-stopping *Scooby Doo*.

It takes a special person to turn adversity and struggle into something positive. How do you perceive setbacks: as obstacles or opportunities?

Run with perseverance the race...before us. (Hebrews 12:1)

God, enable each of us to overcome adversity with love.

God Told Her to Smile

Two years ago a college student's mother suffered a heart attack. Normally, the young woman went through the day with a smile, but that day she walked with sad eyes and silent prayers.

Then, while waiting for a bus, an older woman turned to her and asked if she'd had a rough day. She nodded. The older woman said she had a good heart and a beautiful smile and that she should keep smiling no matter what.

Though their conversation was brief and they never saw each other again, the college student felt she had received a message from God, saying, "I am listening. You are not alone." When she arrived home, her mother's health was better, and she couldn't help but smile.

When days are hard to get through, keep a smile on your face and remember that God is with you. Perhaps He'll even send someone to revive your faith.

Because you have made the...Most High your dwelling place...He will command His angels concerning you to guard you in all your ways. (Psalm 91:9,11)

Eternal Father, grant me the sensitivity to recognize Your messengers and the strength to smile through trying times.

Going Green

Many people are now considering the impact of global warming and how they can make a difference. One world-wide movement is often referred to as *going green*.

Going green means that people try to reduce or eliminate carbon dioxide emissions and their use of gasoline and electricity. They even grow their own food or buy locally.

Here are five tips on saving the environment while saving money:

- Grow some vegetables, fruits, and herbs. Or, buy them at a local farm or farmers' market.
- Create a five year plan to reduce your household's carbon emissions.
- Carpool or use public transportation; vote and lobby for increased funding for handicapped accessible public transportation.
- Use the sun: dry laundry on a clothesline.
- Clean up and re-green your neighborhood.

The world can be a better place, one household at a time.

Discussion...and counsel precedes every undertaking. (Sirach 37:16)

Inspire our efforts to "go green," Lord of the Harvest.

First Woman Wins Computing Award

Septuagenarian Frances E. Allen is the first woman to receive the prestigious Turing Award in computing. It's named for Alan M. Turing, a noted British mathematician.

Along with the accolades came prize-winnings of $100,000 for Allen, a long-time IBM employee. She is recognized as an inspirational mentor to younger researchers and a leader within the computer community. "Fran Allen's work has led to remarkable advances in compiler design and machine architecture that are at the foundation of modern high-performance computing," said awards committee chair Ruzena Bajcsy.

Allen was also the first woman to be named an IBM Fellow. In 2000 the company created the Frances E. Allen Women in Technology Mentoring Award, naming her its first recipient.

Allen said it was "high time for a woman" to win the Turing prize—although "that's not why I got it," she added.

Achieve all you can—and recognize the accomplishments of others.

For everything there is a season, and a time for every matter under heaven. (Ecclesiastes 3:1)

You are the author of women's and men's intellectual achievements, God. Remind us to celebrate Your gifts.

Cleaning up the Bronx

The Waterbury LaSalle Community Association is cleaning up graffiti in the suburban-like northeast Bronx.

One of the Association's volunteers is octogenarian Douglas Clarke, a retired transit worker. He drives through the neighborhoods of Pelham Bay, Country Club and Throgs Neck, looking for graffiti defaced mailboxes. Then, using quick-drying paint, he restores them to a uniform USPS mail-box-green.

Clarke, who sometimes has to repaint the same mailbox time after time, says of the vandals' work, "Sometimes it comes right back, but I've just got to keep painting."

He has the right idea. Do all that you can to keep your community beautiful and to eliminate blight. That begins with your home or apartment. Teach this to your children and young relatives, too. After all, it's your—and their—home and neighborhood! Be proud of it!

The necessities of life are water, bread, and clothing, and also a house to assure privacy. (Sirach 29:21)

Jesus of Nazareth, Son of Joseph and Mary, encourage children and adults to maintain their home or apartment and to preserve or improve their neighborhood.

Travel Souvenirs

Writer Rachel Weingarten, who travels frequently for work, collects "the best of other cultures"—souvenirs she calls them—and incorporates these into her daily life. Here are some of her souvenirs:

- Eat Mediterranean—a diet rich in fruits, vegetables, cereals, fish and olive oil, but sparing in dairy products and meat.

- Turn off the lights; put on a sweater (or wear cotton depending on the season); use energy-saving appliances.

- Be less obsessed with plans and schedules. Make time for doing nothing.

- Learn to live minimally. You'll have less space to clean, heat, decorate and furnish.

- Pause to share whatever little or much you have from your heart.

Find your own unique place; your personal "valley of love and delight" by listening to others' wisdom as well as your body's and soul's.

Take care! Be on your guard against all kinds of greed; for one's life does not consist in the abundance of possessions. (Luke 12:15)

Redeemer, help us to gain a richer, truer, more human life; a simpler life.

When You're Called to Help

When six New York City transit workers reported for work one January morning, they had no idea that they'd be hailed as heroes before the day was over.

They spotted a distressed middle-aged man walking along the subway tracks which run on the Williamsburg Bridge between Manhattan and Brooklyn. The man, screaming that his wife had died and that he wanted to be with her, climbed over the guard railings and threatened to jump into the East River below.

Train operator Aikido Sticatto told him, "If your wife was a strong lady she would not want you to take this way out."

Track inspector Thomas Bodai got close enough to grab the man so they could pull him to safety. Later Bodai said, "The goodness inside you takes over. You just do what you have to."

Life always surprises us. Be ready to do your best.

Christ will Himself restore, support, strengthen, and establish you. To Him be the power forever and ever. Amen. (1 Peter 5:10-11)

Prepare me, Holy Spirit, to answer Your call whenever and wherever You want me.

The Power of Stories

Writer Vinita Hampton Wright believes stories teach her to pay attention. When she faced problems in her writing, she found that "it was only after I paid attention—a practice that involves focus and calm—that I was able to see the answer."

It is not only the writer who benefits from attention, but also the reader. Have you ever read something without paying attention early on and paid the price later when, in an important scene, you cannot recall who a character is? Not to mention subtleties that are missed because of poor attention.

This is not to say that the writer punishes us for not paying attention. It is more that attention is a discipline with great rewards. When we give our minds the space and time to do their work, they will reward us later.

My child, be attentive to my words; incline your ear to my sayings. (Proverbs 4:20)

As I seek You in Your Word, Father, may my mind be open and my quality of attention be high.

Relationship Maintenance 101

Relationships, whether a friendship or a marriage, are rather like cars—to run smoothly and last for many years, they require maintenance. Here are some suggestions for Relationship Maintenance 101 from *Marriage Magazine:*

- Talk about everything that is important to you. Do not keep secrets.
- You needn't always agree, but you must listen and keep your heart open to your friend or spouse.
- Resolve differences ASAP. Don't let them simmer because that kills relationships from the inside out.
- Do not run away physically or emotionally when a problem or challenge arises.
- Neither live in the past nor dwell on what "might" happen. The present is enough.

Love one another, because love is from God; everyone who loves is born of God and knows God....for God is love. (1 John 4:7,8)

God, bless us with mutually loving friendships and marriages.

A Treat for the Ages

The next time you enjoy chocolate or cocoa, think about that treat.

Originally found growing in the rainforests of Central America, the cacao trees provide the pods with seeds that become chocolate. The Mayans and Aztecs added spices and made an unsweetened beverage. With the arrival of the Spanish, the pods found their way to Europe where they were mixed with sugar to make sweet cocoa.

Today, most of the world's cacao is grown on small family farms in West Africa. Pods are hand-harvested; the seeds are removed, boxed, covered with banana leaves and fermented to intensify the chocolate taste. Then the seeds are dried in the sun, bagged and sent to chocolate manufacturers for roasting and processing.

Let's appreciate the human labor that goes into providing our food and drink—and, above all, the divine labor of our Creator.

I took them up in My arms...I led them with cords of human kindness, with bands of love. I was to them like those who lift infants to their cheeks. I bent down to them and fed them. (Hosea 11:3,4)

Father, Your gifts overwhelm us. Thank You for Your loving bounty.

Less Glamorous Service

Translating thought into action can at times seem impossible. Equipped with grand ideas but lacking the commitment and confidence to realize them, one can easily grow discouraged.

Not so with a church youth group in Nevada. They paired their desire to make a difference with their ability to see even the smallest needs: they found out that homeless people rarely receive gloves, underwear, socks and hats to face the winter cold. So they implemented a clothing drive for just these items. It was such a success, now it's a tradition there.

Consider: there are few things more humble than socks and underwear. Those are very basic, boring, little things. But the fact that people don't ignore their neighbors' need and do something about it is extraordinary. What small project is asking for your attention and creative action?

Truly I tell you, just as you did it to one of the least of these, who are members of my family, you did it to me. (Matthew 25:40)

God, motivate me to care greatly about the seemingly little things I can do for others, because they matter.

Seeing the Face of the Poor

The poor are with us—not only in distant countries—but in America's neighborhoods. Poverty is a family struggling on minimum wage salaries; an elderly woman trying to get by on Social Security; or a homeless veteran with mental health problems who's living on the streets.

We can help by staying informed about relevant issues and legislation and then letting government officials know where we stand. We can also volunteer with church or community outreach programs, shelters, food banks, etc.

The Rev. Martin Luther King, Jr., said, "We are called to play the Good Samaritan on life's roadside; but...one day the whole Jericho road must be transformed so that men and women will not be beaten and robbed as they make their journey through life. True compassion is more than flinging a coin to a beggar; it understands that an edifice that produces beggars needs restructuring."

"Which...do you think, was a neighbor to the man who fell into the hands of the robbers?" He said, "The one who showed him mercy." Jesus said to him, "Go and do likewise." (Luke 10:36-37)

Merciful Father, remind us that we have a responsibility to act with true compassion.

For the Guy or Gal Who Has It All

Ever feel stumped at gift-giving time? Choosing the right gift is especially difficult when the recipient has abundant material possessions.

Paige and Matt Rodgers spent a decade buying expensive gifts for one another. Finally, an online search provided an innovative and charitable alternative: a charitable donation in a loved one's name.

Since the Rodgers' work schedules make volunteering difficult, Paige Rodgers was delighted to discover she can help others through the click of a computer mouse. For a recent holiday, she purchased computer training for school children in Sierra Leone, in her husband's name.

Matt Rodgers, who is the first to admit his "closet is full," was thrilled. "This was incredibly creative, and so appropriate to my interests," he said.

There are those who can give their time, and those who can give their money. The needy can benefit from the efforts of both.

A generous person has cause to rejoice. (Sirach 40:14)

Help me be generous, Jesus.

Prayerful Healing

In a fast-paced world it's easy to rely on doctors for diagnoses, the pharmaceutical industry for quick cures, and psychologists for stress relief and mental health. However, even science has its limits, and where technology ends, faith continues.

Harvard University studies show that "prayer literally does the body good" and promotes healing. Intercessory prayer, for instance, "can improve the outcome for patients with heart disorders."

It has been proven that faith does indeed extend life. "According to researchers, churchgoers had healthier immune systems than those who didn't attend services regularly."

When you're feeling helpless, ill, or stressed, you can go to the doctor if need be. But don't forget to pray for yourself and your loved ones.

In fact, pray always and everywhere for everything and everyone, including yourself.

(Jesus) would withdraw to deserted places and pray. (Luke 5:16)

Remind me to pray always, Jesus, prayerful Son of the Covenant.

A Gift of Song

God blessed John Baptist Nguyen Tien Sang with a beautiful voice. As a young man, he earned a music degree. Then he decided to become a priest. Father Sang now ministers to people in three parishes in his native Vietnam.

He has a special housing ministry to help poor people build their own houses. He pays for the $350 to $400 worth of building materials for a home through the sale in of CDs of him singing hymns. The family provides labor and the rest of the costs. Thus far, he's helped build 30 houses.

"God gave me a fine voice," he says, "and I want to use it to earn money to help my poor parishioners."

God calls us to ministry whether we're ordained or not. The apostle Paul, for example, supported himself as a tentmaker while preaching the Gospel. How best can you use God's gifts to serve His people?

Paul...found...Aquila...with his wife Priscilla...and because he was of the same trade, he stayed with them, and they worked together — by trade they were tentmakers. (Acts 18:1,2,3)

Divine Master, show me how to use the talents You've given me for the welfare of Your people.

In the Best Interest of His Community

Entrepreneur Paul Storch's company designs and manufactures custom-made refrigerators that serve a variety of industries, from hospitals to food vendors—hardly a commonplace commodity. Yet, as a business owner, Storch faces a dilemma nearly every business owner faces: the need to maximize the quality of his products while minimizing his costs.

But when faced with the possibility of having to outsource his labor force to keep costs down, Storch was determined to find another solution.

Storch knew that producing his refrigerators locally would not only serve his customers through faster delivery, but also help his community. He invested a sizable sum of his own money—matched by a New York state grant—to develop a skills training program for local workers. Today, residents in Storch's Bronx neighborhood remain the bulk of his company's work staff.

Support your own local economy whenever possible. It's one way to be a good neighbor to others.

You shall love your neighbor as yourself: I am the Lord. (Leviticus 19:18)

Remind me that I am part of a community of many, Father God.

Working Together

People often believe that different religions cannot work together or be amicable.

That's not the case in Franklin Park, Pennsylvania, with neighboring Sts. John and Paul Catholic Church and New Heights Church of God. Each needed a new building: Sts. John and Paul for 1900 families; New Heights for 150.

Parishioners from Sts. John and Paul contributed expertise in real estate, construction, development and law. New Heights signed over its property to Sts. John and Paul. Sts. John and Paul found a 12-acre parcel for New Heights, bought it and built the Protestant church. Because parishioners donated many of the services, the project cost $200,000 less than budgeted.

The pastor of Sts. John and Paul, Rev. Joseph McCaffrey, calls this cooperation "a beautiful example of ecumenism."

Working together to resolve a problem means deciding to grow in tolerance.

Who, then, are you to judge your neighbor? (James 4:12)

Jesus, faithful Son of the Covenant, remind us to cultivate tolerance, respect and knowledge across denominational and religious lines.

For Seniors' Mental Health

Can family and friends help seniors avoid Alzheimer's-like dementia?

A study from the Rush University Medical Center in Chicago led researchers to conclude that long-term lonely people might just be under enough stress to speed the aging of their brains.

The loneliest study participants appeared to be at increased risk of developing memory loss and confusion, two hallmarks of Alzheimer's disease and other dementias.

So, seniors and others, sign up for that class. Join that garden club. Play bingo. Engage the world around you in whatever way possible.

And, as much as possible, stay connected to your family and friends.

Those who live many years should rejoice in them all. (Ecclesiastes 11:8)

Abba, help the aged find remedies for their isolation.

Learning from Others' Wisdom

If you spend time seeking the meaning of life, you're certainly not alone.

Dag Hammarskjold, the second Secretary General of the United Nations, wrote about what he'd learned in his book *Markings*. His father's family taught him "that no life was more satisfactory than one of self-less service to your country—or humanity." From his mother's family he gained a belief that "in the very radical sense of the Gospels, all...were equals as children of God."

He came to appreciate that we can "live a life of active social service in full harmony with (oneself) as a member of the community of the spirit" through the writings of religious mystics.

We have the chance to learn from so many people. Yet putting this knowledge to work for the good of others as well as ourselves, takes daily determination. Without it, we will never completely discover the true meaning of our lives.

When the Spirit of truth comes, He will guide you into all the truth. (John 16:13)

Open my mind and my heart to Your wisdom, Holy Spirit, wherever I may find it.

Working for a Cause

Many Haitian children born with HIV/AIDS are orphaned by the disease. Others are abandoned. They live on the street without adult supervision or medical care and are malnourished.

Trisha and Ray Comfort from Edisto Beach, South Carolina, worked to change that. First they took in a street kid with advanced AIDS, TB, pneumonia, scabies, malnutrition and a balance and coordination disorder. That child inspired them to resurrect a three bedroom house as *Kay Konfo* (Comfort House), an orphanage for these children. In turn, that led a hospital just a few miles away to start a children's AIDS program.

The Comforts introduce the children to prayers before meals and before bed; and also Sunday worship. They expect their staff to be models of Christian values. They also teach the children not to steal, lie or disrespect their elders.

How can you help the poor and sick, especially children?

Religion...is this: to care for orphans and widows in their distress. (James 1:27)

Gentle Jesus, help us be agents of Your loving mercy for orphans and widows.

Where Are You Going?

Have you ever placed an order at a restaurant and told the waiter or waitress not to give you mayonnaise or whatever on your sandwich only to have it turn up anyway?

There's a good reason, according to Jack Canfield and Mark Hanson writing in *The Aladdin Factor.* "Ask for what you want, not for what you don't want. When you tell someone what you don't want, their mind creates a picture of the words you use. Psychologists tell us the unconscious mind filters out all negative words. Now you can see why it is important to ask for what you want instead of what you don't want."

Staying positive is key in so many ways. While you certainly need to recognize problems and deal with them, it's much more important to focus on what you want and where you're going than dwelling on any obstacles in your path.

Hope does not disappoint us. (Romans 5:5)

Merciful Lord, keep my spirit centered on You. Keep me close to Your heart so that I may share Your courage and vision.

Dancing to Understanding

When famed Russian ballerina Marina Leonova, head of the Moscow State Academy of Choreography, spoke at the National Arts Club in the summer of 2007, it was to extend an invitation.

The Moscow-based Bolshoi Ballet Academy was offering a master class to New York City kids, hoping to turn them into "dancing diplomats" in five weeks.

"The arts are the best bridge between countries," explained Alden James, president of the National Arts Club, who saw the program as a United Nations-type endeavor. "When we unite, we enter a much more peaceful world."

The classes would introduce a very different style of teaching, in the Russian classical ballet tradition, explained Leonova. "We want American kids to be introduced to our art and culture," she added. Observed James, "Our teachers and our students will be the best ambassadors."

Often the differences between us seem less distinct when we stand—or dance—side-by-side.

Of Zion it shall be said, "This one and that one were born in it"...Singers and dancers alike say, "All my springs are in you." (Psalm 87:5,7)

The beauty around us gives praise to You, Lord, and commands us to offer You thanks.

It Is Easy Being Green

Remember Kermit, that cute little green frog on TV's *Sesame Street*, who sang, "It's Not Easy Being Green"? Environmental conservation experts would disagree with him. "Being green" is easier than we might think when it comes to caring for our environment. Radical life changes aren't needed. Try these simple steps:

- Clean up naturally. Household chemicals contribute to pollution. Use products like vinegar or lemon juice when possible.

- Junk your junk mail. More than annoying, it destroys trees and pollutes the environment during the printing process.

- Dim the lights. Turn off lights when not in use. Use energy-conscious electric bulbs.

- Eat more fresh vegetables and fruit. You are purchasing products without packaging, saving trees and petroleum, and decreasing packaging that cannot decompose in landfills.

Make an effort to be green today.

Let us choose what is right. (Job 34:4)

Thank You, Father-Creator, for Your precious Earth! Enlighten our efforts to conserve it.

Let It Snow

Many people who live where snow is a regular part of their winter have something of a love-hate relationship with it.

The beauty of a snowfall and the fun of making snowmen and snow angels are balanced by all the shoveling and the slipping and sliding as you walk or drive after a snow storm.

You know that snow is a type of frozen precipitation, but you might not realize that snowflakes are microscopic specks containing many ice crystals that form inside a cloud. While most flakes are a hexagon, they can also form plates, columns, needles or branches. Perhaps most interestingly, no two are alike.

As for the white color of snow, the fact is that visible sunlight is white, and snow is a natural material that both absorbs and reflects light.

God provides such breadth of beauty in His Creation that we can never stop feeling wonder—if only we keep our eyes and spirits open.

From the greatness and beauty of created things comes a corresponding perception of their Creator. (Wisdom of Solomon 13:5)

Your love and loveliness astound us as we look at this world You have given us as our home, Beautiful Creator.

An Exemplary Life

Becoming a judge is generally enough to impress most people. Consider, however, attaining such success as a black woman in the 1930s in the United States.

That's exactly what the Honorable Jane Bolin, the country's first female African-American judge, did in 1939 when New York City Mayor Fiorello LaGuardia appointed her to Family Court. Judge Bolin served four 10-year terms.

Judge Bolin was also the first black woman to graduate from Yale Law School; the first black woman to join the New York Bar Association; the first black woman to work New York City's own legal department.

As a judge, Bolin ended the assignment of probation officers by race and the placement of children in child-care agencies by ethnicity. She said it was a delusion to think "there is superiority among human beings by reasons solely of color, race or religion." She lived that belief all her 98 years.

Do we honor the equality of all human beings?

Deborah, a prophetess, wife of Lappidoth, was judging Israel...and the Israelites came up to her for judgment. (Judges 4:4,5)

Father God, inspire women.

In Living Waters

Orthodox Jewish women have practiced it for centuries, albeit quietly. Says one rabbi, "Even children don't know where Mommy goes. It's the most personal part of a woman's life, and one of the most secret, undisclosed practices."

The practice is the ancient Jewish ritual of mikvah, or full immersion in "living" waters. For married women of childbearing age, the tradition has a special significance: a monthly sacred bath to sanctify their return to intimate relations with their husbands, it represents compliance with the Jewish laws of "family purity."

Today, the ritual may seem outdated. But believers say the tradition enhances marital harmony, passion and mutual respect.

Tolerance stems from information, understanding and respect. Delve into the significance of customs that seem strange to you. With understanding, you will come to respect and appreciate the traditions of others.

After eight days...it was time to circumcise the child; and He was called Jesus. ...For their purification according to the law of Moses, they brought Him up to Jerusalem to present Him to the Lord. (Luke 2:21,22)

Jesus who lived and died an observant Jew, remind us to respect others' religious beliefs.

Patience in the Waiting Room

Patience is a virtue. But what happens when you can't be patient anymore?

Often, in doctors' offices, patients must wait long periods of time until they are called for their examination or consultation. It can be hard to keep your patience when the time for your appointment comes and goes and you're still waiting. Here are some helpful tips to distract yourself and make the most of your time:

- Bring something that will take your mind off the wait, say a book.
- Remember why you are there.
- Say a prayer of patience for yourself and others.

These three simple steps can make a long wait much easier to endure.

**Endure everything with patience.
(Colossians 1:11)**

Remind doctors and their staffs as well as patients to respect the time of all, Lord God.

From Recycling to Reading

Ever notice how one good idea often leads to another?

Stockton Springs, Maine, never had a library. Then the small town located on Penobscot Bay acquired a large house once owned by a sea captain, and the local historical society took it over.

"The library was sort of a spin-off idea," said Basil Staples who, with his wife Mary, helped found the library which is on the first floor of the building. Since 2001, it has been run by about 20 volunteers with $3,500 a year provided by the town. That's when the Staples came up with a plan for additional income—recycling.

The town didn't have a center to recycle cans and bottles, so now people leave these items in a cart in front of the library, raising about $3,000 a year for the institution.

Neighbors can accomplish a great deal by working together—and by being creative. Do what you can to improve your community.

To each is given the manifestation of the Spirit for the common good. (1 Corinthians 12:7)

Endow me with Your own spirit of creativity and wisdom, Almighty Father.

Ways to Help

If you think you don't have the money, time, talent, or whatever you imagine it takes to help others, think again. And think s-m-a-l-l.

As small as a pair of socks.

Inspired to help others by the work of JoAnn Cayce, who has spent decades as a volunteer serving the needs of impoverished neighbors in Arkansas, writer Joan Wester Anderson decided to make her own contribution.

Anderson, who often writes about angels and has her own website, asked her readers to send socks to Cayce. They responded with more than 25,000 pairs. "Packages of socks, clothes and money arrived from around the world," says Anderson.

Meanwhile, Cayce's grandson Daniel has done his part by collecting and distributing blankets and household goods. For his efforts he received the 2004 Young Adult National Caring Award.

Every effort, large or small, from young or old, can help.

Every generous act of giving, with every perfect gift, is from above, coming down from the Father. (James 1:17)

Inspire us to simple acts of generosity, Jesus.

The Path to Leadership

Professors Joseph Skelly, Kathy Ingram, and Dale Patrias are professors at the College of Mount Saint Vincent in Bronx County, New York, and they teach students to become leaders.

In the leadership integrated course at the college, these three teachers offer their opinions and encourage students to become leaders. Skelly, Ingram, and Patrias assign one significant task. They ask their students to perform four hours of service and to write about it. Although this is a requirement to pass the course, many students walk away with newfound personal involvement with people who are in need.

Skelly says, "Today, many young people, inspired by Jesus' example, have embraced the fundamentals of servant leadership. They realize that putting others first is one way to live out the Golden Rule, and to grow closer to God."

Everyone can become a leader with the right opportunity. Are you ready to become one?

I have given you an example. (Acts 20:35)

Lord, help us not only to be Your followers, but also leaders who can make a difference.

Living Whole, Whole Living

Think of the popularity of *whole* these days in company names such as Whole Foods and Whole Earth, or as desirable things such as whole grains or whole buildings, for example.

More than these, *whole, holistic*—meaning healthy, unhurt, entire—should define our living. Here are some thoughts:

- Loving acts begin at home but ripple outward.
- Transitions are opportunities to look at who you are and where you're going.
- Let go of what you don't need to make space for what you want.
- Pay attention to those desires for change which show up in your body and your thoughts.
- Help others because they need it, not just because you want to help.
- Giving is key to a happier, healthier life.
- Teach what you know; and discover what you're ready to learn.

A healthy life comes from better choices. Choose wisely.

Commit your work to the Lord, and your plans will be established. (Proverbs 16:3)

Show me how to live a whole life as the person You want me to be, Gracious Creator.

Advocate for Lepers and Outcasts

As a boy he'd shocked his Brahmin family by playing with the servants' children and those of low caste. As a lawyer his outrage at social injustice grew along with his wealth and status.

Then one night Merlidhar Devidas Amte passed Tulshiram, a rain-soaked, naked, fingerless, maggot-ridden leper. He ran home, fearing infection. But prodded by his conscience, Amte returned and personally fed and housed Tulshiram until he died.

Then Amte went to work at leprosy clinics and studied leprosy at the Calcutta School of Tropical Medicine. In 1951, he, his wife and their children, six leprosy patients, a lame cow and a dog established Anandvan, a lepers' commune. Now more than 50 years later, Anandvan houses 3,000 mostly disfigured, crippled, blind or deaf people.

People continue to be isolated and disowned because of prejudice and misinformation. What can you do to restore their human dignity?

Jesus...touched him, and said..."Be made clean!" Immediately the leprosy left him. (Mark 1:41-42)

What does it mean for me to reach out to the outcast, scorned or rejected person, Jesus?

Women: Givers to the World

Marsha Wallace of Greenville, South Carolina, like many other working women and mothers of families, found herself losing touch with friends and concerns outside her profession.

Wallace felt she could do better. She formed a potluck dinner group for the women of the town which has grown into the Dining for Women program. Instead of going to an expensive restaurant for a "girls' night out," the women bring in home-cooked food. The money they would have spent on dinner is donated instead to families in need.

Now there are many chapters of Dining for Women across the country. One woman's idea to bring together her friends and make a contribution has helped make a change for the better. What can you do to help your neighbors—and yourself, too?

Just as the body without the spirit is dead, faith without works is also dead. (James 2:26)

Inspire us to effect even a tiny change for the better within our milieu, Holy Wisdom.

On the Seventh Day, We Rested

When Lynne Baab and her husband, who are Christians, moved to Tel Aviv, Israel, they found that everything closed from sunset Friday to sunset Saturday in observance of the Sabbath.

At first they struggled to fill the time. But after a while they decided to relax and enjoy the day. They read, walked and talked. She wrote long letters while he went bird-watching.

"Sometimes we prayed together," Baab explained. "We simply slowed down. We rested in God's love and experienced His grace."

This couple kept the Sabbath slow and work-free even after they returned to the United States. "It remains a day to rest in God's goodness," said Baab, who went on to write a book called *Sabbath Keeping*.

Every one of us needs time to slow down the pace—and to enjoy family and friends, or just time alone. What better day than the Sabbath—the day on which God Himself rested.

God...rested on the seventh day from all the work that He had done. So God blessed the seventh day. (Genesis 2:2-3)

Blessed are You, O Lord our God, who has commanded us to observe a weekly Sabbath of rest.

He Never Gave Up

"Hope Runs in Our Family." These are the words of neurologist and father, John Castaldo.

Castaldo's son David was in a car accident at age sixteen that left him in a coma. For Castaldo, it was a new feeling to be on the receiving end of bad news. Castaldo is a doctor who often has to deliver news—good or bad—to patients' families.

While Castaldo felt that the doctors were giving up hope that his son would wake up, he never did. On the tenth day of his son's coma, he asked him to raise two fingers to show he could hear. "Two fingers shot up from Dave's right hand in the form of a victory sign," Castaldo later said.

In time David Castaldo recovered enough to finish high school and college. He now repairs and rebuilds computers.

Hope and faith can help guide us through any crisis.

Rejoice in hope. (Romans 12:12)

Holy Spirit, fill me to the brim with resolute faith and hope.

Courage and Conscience

Maintaining the courage of your convictions isn't easy. That may even be more true when you're dealing with life-or-death situations involving a whole nation.

Abraham Lincoln led a divided United States of America through the bitter Civil War. He was plagued by corrupt officials, incompetent generals and constant criticism. It's clear that while he appreciated the approval of others, Lincoln did not depend on it.

"I do the very best I can," he said. "I mean to keep going. If the end brings me out all right, then what is said against me won't matter. If I'm wrong, ten angels swearing I was right won't make a difference."

God entrusts us with power of mind and spirit. Whenever we act conscientiously, we strengthen our moral sense and become better people.

(The Lord) created humankind...and He left them...their own free choice. If you choose, you can keep the commandments. (Sirach 15:14-15)

Divine Father, lead me in making wise and just choices today and every day.

The Garden of the Lord

A biography of Charles Schulz, author of the classic comic-strip *Peanuts,* revealed how his life, like our own, was many-layered and complicated. Recalling his life, one friend said, "You could see the bitterness in him. Nothing in all of his 77 years had been resolved."

Whether or not Charles Schulz felt the anguish of resentment, it's certainly true that bitterness often follows injury or injustice. It's said to "take root" in our hearts and is frequently connected with exaggerating our hurts and not resolving them.

All of us experience injustice, and so it follows that all of us are in jeopardy of becoming embittered. But if we have the strength to confront injustice—to resolve it and not imagine that only we suffer, but everyone around us does, too—then we uproot bitterness. We clear the soil for a garden of justice in our own lives, yielding the fruits of justice to share with others.

The Lord will comfort Zion; He will...make her wilderness like Eden, her desert like the garden of the Lord. (Isaiah 51:3)

Dear Jesus, be my Gardener and I Your helper. Let no bitterness take root in me; may my life bear Your justice.

A Genuine Valentine

The Sullivans were trying to stay sane between work and two toddlers. Through an agency they hired their first au pair, Andrea Nieto Hernandez. Hernandez charmed the toddlers. She also programmed their computers and electronics; assembled furniture; and fixed the toilet!

But then she started experiencing jaw pain. The Sullivan's dentist and two doctors checked. Hernandez had a C.T. scan and two biopsies and was diagnosed with a non-malignant, lemon-sized schwannoma. The tumor impinged on her brain and optic nerves.

The Sullivans' neighbors worried about how they'd cope without her. One said they'd "have to send her home."

Instead, on the night before her surgery, Hernandez and the Sullivans dined at an expensive restaurant. Her agency's insurance paid for the tumor's removal. And her mother and brother stayed with her at the Sullivans during her convalesce.

The best St. Valentine's Day gifts are the ones that continue to give day after day.

Bear one another's burdens, and...you will fulfill the law of Christ. (Galatians 6:2)

Whose burden can I help lift from their shoulders, God?

Best Friends — Unconditional Love

Did you know that dogs can encourage beginning readers? Teachers often pair students and have them read aloud to each other. But struggling readers often hesitate over words and their student-partners become impatient.

But not Ruby, a long-haired dachshund, and one of thousands of certified therapy dogs who help youngsters learn to read. Once a week Ruby visits a Schenectady, New York, school and sits with a student who reads aloud. She neither judges nor corrects; the student has an accepting audience.

Barnaby, a small terrier, helps Eileen Brennan teach reading. One of her students had avoided reading aloud for nine weeks. Then Brennan suggested he read aloud to Barnaby. The boy read while pointing to the words and looking at the pictures. Eventually, he was reading smoothly, fluently, eagerly.

Dogs' uncritical, non judgmental nature helps make them lovable. Now if only we humans could be less critical and judgmental!

Do not judge so that you may not be judged. (Matthew 7:1)

From holding myself and others to standards that You do not, Gentle Jesus, deliver me.

In Foreign Service

Ed Mahoney could have spent his retirement in golfing and other leisure activities, but traveling to Guatemala changed all that.

Mahoney's first trip left him eager to learn more about the country's people and culture. On his second visit, he returned with a more serious mission: to volunteer at a daycare center. What he saw changed the way he looked at the world and himself. "I never realized anything like this existed," he said, referring to the level of poverty and need. "When you see it for the first time, it takes your breath away."

Before long, Mahoney was part of Safe Passage, an organization serving the children and families who scavenge Guatemala City's dumps for food and clothing. During his years of volunteer work, the number of children it serves has grown from 185 to 550, and there's now a home for victims of abuse and neglect.

Examine your role in this world of ours.

Whoever welcomes this child in My name welcomes Me, and whoever welcomes Me welcomes the One who sent Me; for the least among all of you is the greatest. (Luke 9:48)

Holy Spirit, remind us that in whatever way we help children we help the Child Jesus.

Gratitude, a Close Relative

"Gratitude is not only the greatest of virtues, but the parent of all the others," wrote Cicero. Though it is not itself a fruit of the spirit, it is related to them.

A pastor once compared gratitude to eyeglasses: it's only with a disposition of thankfulness that we can see the events of our lives clearly. But how does that apply to someone suffering from the loss of a loved one?

One young woman whose father had died said, "To be grateful for this loss, which had altered my future and threatened to change everything about me and all my relationships, seemed absurd. But I have found it to be true: the more I can thank God for the love and strength I find in Him, the more I can become the daughter my dad and my heavenly Father raised me to be."

Ask God to bless your heart with gratitude.

With gratitude in your hearts sing psalms, hymns, and spiritual songs to God. (Colossians 3:16)

God, thank You for today, for loving me, for hearing my prayers.

Have Your Say

We all want to be heard. Now more ordinary people can be, thanks to StoryCorps, started by radio producer David Isay in 2003. The project allows family and friends to record the voices of their loved ones responding to their questions.

"How did you meet Mom?"

"Does the cancer scare you?"

The first StoryCorps mobile booth, a miniature radio recording studio, was set up in New York City. Today, two travel the country.

Anyone can sign up to do a 40 minutes interview in the soundproof booth. Participants get a recording of their interview. With their permission, a copy is sent to the Library of Congress.

Isay believes that "StoryCorps tells people they matter and they won't be forgotten."

Let the people in your life know they matter.

Consider the ravens; they neither sow nor reap, they have neither storehouse nor barn, and yet God feeds them. Of how much more value are you than the birds! (Luke 12:24)

Abba, remind me of my infinite value.

Addressing Needs Together

In Michigan, one urban parish and one suburban parish united to provide illiterate children with a resource for changing the status quo.

Since the needs of inner-city parishes tend to outstrip their resources, the churches took an innovative approach and established the ministry they call Bound Together. Volunteers focus on breaking the cycle of illiteracy that affects many of the children. They also use the arts—including theater, dance, film and writing—to encourage youngsters to think critically.

Delivering a big ministry from small means is nothing new for followers of Jesus. God chose to deliver mercy through the hands of Jesus *and* His disciples.

What innovative ways can we find to multiply our resources, so that we can change the status quo?

Very truly, I tell you, the one who believes in Me will also do the works that I do and, in fact, will do greater works than these, because I am going to the Father. (John 14:12)

Jesus, if there is injustice, I want to right it— not alone, but as part of Your body.

The Guitar That Was a Gun

When Colombian musician César López plays at anti-violence events, his guitar is a gun—or at least it once was, an AK-47 rifle, to be exact.

In early 2003, not long after a bloody terrorist attack in his homeland, López noticed that a soldier held his rifle in the same way he held his guitar. The first *escopetarra*—*escopeta* is shotgun in Spanish, and *guitarra,* guitar—was produced a few months later.

For López, the gun-turned-guitar represents the union between humanity's ugliest invention and one of its most beautiful. He has given *escopetarras* to international artists who are working for peace.

"The fact that a weapon is transformed in such a radical way speaks of the possibility the whole planet has to change, even it if seems absurd," López explains.

Change is always possible. It begins with an open spirit, an open mind and an open heart.

Look! On the mountains the feet of one who brings good tidings, who proclaims peace! (Nahum 1:15)

Hear our prayers, Lord, and show us how to make peace, not war.

Gaining God, Losing Weight

If you want to achieve something important you probably pray about it, right? So why should weight loss be different?

Several faith-based weight loss programs exist to help people reach their goal of better health and respect for their bodies. One program called First Place was begun by Carole Lewis about 25 years ago in Houston's First Baptist Church. It asks each participant in the 13-week sessions not only to diet and exercise, but also to attend a weekly Bible Study and weigh-in, to contact another group member weekly for encouragement, and to read the Bible daily.

However, it's important to remember that being thin doesn't equate with being holy or being heavy with being sinful, according to Mary Louise Bringle, a professor of philosophy and theology at North Carolina's Brevard College.

Whatever your aim, turn to God and trust in His help.

Thus says the Lord...who formed you...you are precious in My sight, and honored, and I love you. (Isaiah 43:1,4)

Loving Abba, remind me that You love me completely just as I am.

Letting Go

Children who grow up in dysfunctional families often have psychological scars as adults. Instead of allowing harsh memories to dictate the present and future, author T. Suzanne Eller, who also had a difficult youth, offers these four R's for dealing with a painful past:

- Refocus—on the here and now and how far you've come since those childhood days.
- Be Realistic—and remember good memories, not just bad ones.
- Relent—and find a way to be merciful and let go of the bitterness that prevents your moving on.
- Receive—and allow those who have hurt you to express their love for you, however awkwardly.

You can not undo past wrongs and hurts, but it's possible to move on as an adult. Let God's grace help you.

Jesus said, "Let the little children come to Me, and do not stop them; for it is to such as these that the kingdom of heaven belongs." (Matthew 19:14)

Divine Physician, bring health to men and women suffering the wounds of physical, spiritual and emotional child abuse.

The Bishop and the Egg Timer

"It's a bit weird when you see a bishop handing you an egg timer," conceded Bishop Steven Cottrell, Anglican Bishop of Reading, England. He's written a book, *Do Nothing to Change Your Life,* in which he suggests taking rest and play seriously.

He urges readers to make and take a "happy hour;" a time to initiate an adventure of self-discovery and creativity; a time to sit silently and still. This would, Bishop Cottrell wrote, transform the way they saw life; how they related to God. "By learning to sit still, slow down, by discerning when to shut up and when to speak out," Bishop Cottrell said, "you learn to travel through life differently."

And that's how Bishop Cottrell happened to hand out egg timers to harried commuters at a railroad station. Set the timer to three minutes and do—"well, precisely nothing."

Try it. Today.

Be silent before the Lord God. (Zephaniah 1:7)

Help me take silence, rest and play very seriously, God who came to Elijah as a "sound of sheer silence," and a "still small voice."

Family Reunion

Sometimes it's hard to understand why families are torn apart, and why children are abandoned. But for one family, holding on to hope was all they had.

Jen and Mark Adler of Tomah, Wisconsin, adopted little Tania from a Siberian orphanage, leaving behind her older brothers who could not be located at the time. They had been separated, Tania going to one orphanage, and her brothers Zurik and Chingese going to another. After being adopted, however, Tania could not stop thinking about her brothers. Thanks to her adoptive parents, the two boys have now been reunited with their younger sister and are a part of a loving family.

Like these children, who had lost everything and had been separated and are now together, hold on to hope to make it through.

I have put my hope in the Everlasting...and joy has come to me from the Holy One. (Baruch 4:22)

Keep me resolutely hopeful, Lord of all hope.

A Few Reminders from God

In today's fast paced world, we often forget the true meaning of life. The realities by which God judges us are not those of society. Remember:

- God doesn't worry about your clothes, but whether you've clothed the cold and naked.
- God doesn't want you to only help yourself, but help others.
- God won't ask where you lived, but how you treated your neighbors.
- God doesn't worry about the size of your house, but whether you welcomed all into it.
- He won't ask you how many possessions you kept, but whether you put them before Him.

Lastly, always remember that God doesn't judge us by the way we look, how we dress, or even our skin color. We are all His dearly beloved children. All that matters is that we live our lives with love.

(Jesus) said..."You shall love the Lord your God with all your heart, and with all your soul, and with all your mind. ...You shall love your neighbor as yourself. On these two commandments hang all the law and the prophets."
(Matthew 22:37,39)

Help us live Your law of love, Savior.

Well-Made Wishes

In 1973, Thomas Kelly built a wishing well around an "ugly water spigot" on the land near his home in Dorchester, Massachusetts. Eventually, the people from the neighborhood would go to the well to make a wish and then drop in a coin.

Kelly was not the kind of man to keep the money. Instead, he would empty the well of all the coins and donate them to St. Margaret's Church for the needy people in the community.

Kelly sold the house in 1991 and has since died. But a local woman maintains the well and makes sure that the money goes to the needy in the community.

A good deed can begin with one person and continue with many others. What charitable deed can you do?

**Open your hand to the poor.
(Deuteronomy 15:11)**

Benevolent Father, help us to always remember that it's better to give than to receive.

Count Your Blessings

When Sara-Paige Widener complains about a "bad hair day," she's not really griping at all.

You see, she was a college freshman in 2005 when she was diagnosed with advanced brain cancer. Following chemotherapy, her hair is beginning to grow back.

And the young woman never stopped thinking about others in the same predicament. Widener and her mother, Barbara, were honored on the 2007 Make a Difference Day. According to *USA Today,* "the duo raised $15,000 for treatment of needy and pediatric cancer patients."

Despite her own illness, Widener chose to find joy in living and helping others. If you count your blessings and share them, then even a so called bad-hair day will be a good day.

The good person brings good things out of a good treasure. (Matthew 12:35)

Show us, Divine Physician, how to bring good out of our own sufferings.

Neighborhoods, the Environment for Caring

We do not always know when a neighbor is suffering. But when we *do* see him or her struggle, it's best not to wait to offer our help.

When she saw her recently divorced neighbor battle loneliness and financial problems, Jan Johnson found an answer: she became her neighbor's "resource person." She noticed that her neighbor often couldn't motivate herself to do practical things, so Jan did some of them for her: brought her food, paid her to babysit for her children and encouraged her to take a test for a higher-paying teaching job. "I learned to praise her for her confident moments and walk with her through the discouraging ones," Johnson wrote.

Somehow it can seem so difficult to help those close to us who are in need. But really, it's so simple. What's really hard is seeing someone hurt and letting it stay that way.

How does God's love abide in anyone who has the world's goods and sees a brother or sister in need and yet refuses help? (1 John 3:17)

God, may I be deeply troubled by my neighbors' sufferings, and be thus mobilized to be their present and willing help.

Driving Jesus' Car

For Rev. Jim Ball, his pulpit is parked in front of his townhouse—a custom made hybrid car that is, according to him, the ultimate "What Would Jesus Drive?" vehicle.

Executive director of the nonprofit Evangelical Environmental Network, Rev. Ball and wife Kara drove from Texas east across the Bible Belt to awaken others to the threat of global warming.

The Virginia couple's environmental concern isn't just with cars. It also focuses on how they clean their clothes and home, as well as how they shop for groceries and furniture.

"I'm literally taking Jesus as Lord of my life, of everything," explains Rev. Ball. "There's nothing that falls outside that scope."

May our daily duties always begin with a prayer of thanksgiving to the Creator—and continue with a careful stewardship of His Creation.

Think of us in this way, as servants of Christ and stewards of God's mysteries. Moreover, it is required of stewards that they be found trustworthy. (1 Corinthians 4:1-2)

Gracious Creator, I give thanks for the work of Your hands.

Suitcases for Kids

In 1996, little Aubyn Burnside and her brother Welland learned from their older sister Leslie that many foster children did not have suitcases for their clothes when moving from home to home. The children had only plastic garbage bags to hold their belongings.

The Burnside children decided that instead of allowing young children to experience the shame of carrying their few possessions in garbage bags, they would donate suitcases. This was the start of Suitcases for Kids. In their first year, the organization was able to collect 300 suitcases. The non-profit group is now in all 50 states and many other countries.

With your prayer and action you can support adoption for all children in need of fostering. Providing a suitcase would be a start.

Whoever becomes humble like this child is the greatest in the kingdom of heaven. Whoever welcomes one such child in My Name welcomes Me. (Matthew 18:4-5)

Gentle Jesus, help us show compassion to Your suffering children by our deeds.

Sweet, Sweet Gift

The next time you sit down to a stack of breakfast pancakes, look at the bottle of maple syrup. You know, of course, that it comes from maple trees, but did you ever wonder how tree sap turns into sweet, delicious syrup?

The New England states, New York and several Midwestern states as well as Quebec and Ontario, Canada, are known for the delicacy. There, in early spring, holes are drilled into the black or red sugar maple trees and a tap inserted. At one time buckets were hung from them, but now plastic tubes carry the sap which is then evaporated in large, flat, heated pans. One tree yields about 10 gallons over the course of a month. It takes 30 to 50 gallons of sap to make just one gallon of maple syrup.

Nature provides so many marvelous gifts. Let's enjoy and appreciate them and the Creator who made all things.

Out of the ground the Lord God made to grow every tree that is pleasant to the sight and good for food. (Genesis 2:9)

Your bounty is beyond imagining, Creator. Help me show my appreciation by caring for Your good earth.

Making War Less Ugly

War is an ugly, inhuman thing that people at home can ignore. But soldiers are in the thick of it, putting their lives on the line. While some people prefer to protect themselves from the realities of war, Annie Hassee of Greenwood, Indiana, then ten-years-old, wanted to let a soldier know that she cared.

It started with a class project, when she and her classmates wrote to a soldier in Iraq. When Annie received a response from a wounded soldier, they became pen pals. He told her how grateful he was for her letters, and when he returned home, he not only met her face-to-face, but he honored her by giving her his Purple Heart.

Find a way, as Annie did, to do the right thing by not only thinking, but actually doing something beneficial for someone else; by trying to help someone who truly knows the cost of war.

**There is posterity for the peaceable.
(Psalm 37:37)**

Jesus, Prince of Peace, remind us to "care for him who shall have borne the battle and for his widow, and his orphan" even as we labor for peace.

A New Vision

James Holman's dream to see the world was shattered when he lost his vision in his mid-twenties. But the young British Royal Navy officer's passion for travel remained intact. In fact, he was destined to become known as "The Blind Explorer."

Defying expectations, Holman, who was born in 1786, set off on a series of adventures that ultimately took him from England to Siberia, Africa, South America, Australia, India, Turkey and the Middle East.

Holman blazed new trails and was an inspiration to others. He also proved, contrary to then popular belief, that being blind did not mean being helpless or mentally impaired.

Most of us can see, even if eyeglasses are necessary. But discrimination and prejudice against those with limited or no vision remains. What can you do to make life more respect-filled for blind people and those with impaired sight?

You shall not revile the deaf or put a stumbling block before the blind; you shall fear your God: I am the Lord. (Leviticus 19:14)

Help us to respect the human dignity of people with disabilities, Holy Spirit.

Dewey? Not at This Library

If you go into the newest library in the Phoenix suburb of Gilbert, you won't be able to locate a book using the Dewey Decimal System.

Pushing the trend in some libraries to be more like chain bookstores—complete with easy chairs, coffee bars, and displays of best sellers—this Arizona library has gone a step further. Books here are shelved in "neighborhoods" based on what they are about—like "mystery," "philosophy," "spirituality," and "adult fiction."

"The younger generation is wired differently than people in my generation," observes 69-year-old Harry Courtright, director of the 15-branch Maricopa County Library District which includes the Dewey-free library. "What that tells me is we as librarians have to look at how we present materials that we have for them the way they want it."

No matter the goal in life, how we get there is as important as our arriving.

Keep my steps steady according to Your promise, and never let iniquity have dominion over me. Redeem me from human oppression, that I may keep your precepts. (Psalm 119:133-134)

Open my mind and heart, Master, that I may see the way to best serve You.

Tapestry of History

Born in 1919, Nora Ezell, a daughter of a Birmingham, Alabama steelworker, was a quilter most of her life.

She was known among skilled quilters when, in the 90s, she was commissioned by the Birmingham Civil Rights Institute to produce "A Tribute to the Civil Righters of Alabama."

Through intricate stitching and paneling in the African-American quilting tradition, Ezell created a comprehensive and complex work depicting central moments in the civil rights struggle: images of Rosa Parks refusing to relinquish her bus seat in 1955; the 1965 attack by police on civil rights marchers on Birmingham's Edmund Pettus Bridge.

She said, "I like to put a little bit of me in my quilts because I think this is one thing that lives on after us."

Nora Ezell used her unique craft and talent to bring a critical message to all. How can you employ your talents?

Serve one another with whatever gift each of you has received. (1 Peter 4:10)

God, forbid that we should ever forget the on-going cost of "life, liberty and the pursuit of happiness!"

Shabbat Shalom/Sabbath Peace

Recently, a columnist waxed nostalgic about the "blue law" Sundays of his youth when "you couldn't get an aspirin," and it was "church, long walks, an afternoon meal, a game of catch... baseball on the radio...a book...lazy conversation about nothing that mattered." But no lawn mowing or heavy gardening.

Fast forward to 21st century America. Imagine strict blue laws which could mean all stores, even pharmacies, might be forced to close Fridays (for Muslims), Saturdays (for Jews and Seventh Day Adventists) and Sundays (for Christians). Business, industry, medicine and commerce squeezed into four days!

Now think of the freedom of an internalized Sabbath which you keep because that's how you choose to honor God, not how you obey a law or impose your observances on others.

God give you *Shabbat Shalom*, Sabbath Peace!

The Sabbath was made for humankind, and not humankind for the Sabbath. (Mark 2:27)

Eternal Lord, help me to worship You gladly, freely, from my heart; not because of any law.

A. A.—and a Woman Who Changed Lives

Alcoholics Anonymous began in the 1930's with two men who sought to help themselves—and eventually others—stop drinking. But Bill W. and Dr. Bob, as they're known, had a partner who helped the earliest members get medical care at a time when alcoholism was considered a moral failing, not a disease.

Sister Mary Ignatia Gavin persuaded St. Thomas Hospital in Akron, Ohio, and, later, St. Vincent's in Cleveland, to care for alcoholics starting the 12 Step Program that could change their lives. "We begin where reality begins for the alcoholic," she said. "Reality for the alcoholic is drinking. …The alcoholic is ill, in body, mind, and soul; hence we begin with the physical care."

God loves us and wants the best for our whole being. Look after yourself and your loved ones. Ask God to help you to be the person He wants you to be.

Wine drunk at the proper time and in moderation is rejoicing of heart and gladness of soul. Wine drunk to excess leads to bitterness of spirit, to quarrels and stumbling. (Sirach 31:28-29)

God, grant me the serenity to accept the things I cannot change, courage to change the things I can, and wisdom to know the difference.

Encouraging Your Child's Faith

"We want our children to be gracious and grateful…to have courage in difficult times…to have a sense of joy and purpose," notes Rabbi Sandy Eisenberg Sasso in *Family Circle* magazine.

Pointing out that children "have a conception of God" by age five, Rabbi Sasso suggests these simple ways to deepen and support your child's hunger for mystery, for God:

- Show children what's important by your words and deeds with other people, for example, a homeless person.
- Create family rituals.
- Share your own wonder at creation with your children.
- Invite your children to verbalize their experiences of joy and sorrow.
- Encourage and model times of silence.
- Live your own beliefs.

Remember, belief is a free gift, freely accepted and lived. It's up to parents to model their beliefs.

By grace you have been saved through faith, and this is not your own doing; it is the gift of God. (Ephesians 2:8)

Abba, make my faith fearless, inquiring, loyal and tolerant.

A Community of Elders

Even now in the 21st-century, elderly people are too often considered unable to help themselves, incapable of contributing to society, and befuddled if not senile.

Instead, the elderly should be seen not as helpless, but as wise, people. Mabou, Nova Scotia, Canada, is a Cape Breton Island village where the people are close-knit and keep old traditions alive. If one farmer is having difficulty with his crops, for example, the others come to help.

Lydia McKinnon, upon visiting her mother-in-law in a senior citizens' home there, was surprised to see such personal relationships in the town. McKinnon learned from her that there's even a group of grandmothers who get together every Tuesday to pray for their grandchildren. McKinnon states, "Helping others, I have learned, is truly a way of life in this small Nova Scotia town, passed down through the generations."

Most elderly people are capable, intelligent, and sturdy. Work to end discrimination against the aged.

Rich experience is the crown of the aged, and their boast is the fear of the Lord. (Sirach 25:6)

Remind us to use well the experience and wisdom of the aged, Ancient of Days.

Becoming Whole Again

When a woman is diagnosed with breast cancer, it's a terrifying experience.

For Betsy Carter, a passionate athlete, the idea of losing a breast was beside the point. Carter's problem was "losing my physical confidence, my sense of my body as my best buddy—that was much harder."

Then the arrival of a furry friend gave her a sense of much needed normalcy. Lucy, a Tibetan terrier puppy didn't see Carter as bald or disfigured but as a source of love and attention.

After spending much time with Lucy and regaining her physical abilities, Carter attributes her recovery to the relationship she had with Lucy in helping her to find a wholeness that seemed to be lacking in her recovery process.

Healing love can take many forms.

God anointed Jesus of Nazareth with the Holy Spirit and...He went about doing good and healing all. (Acts 10:38)

Merciful Savior, make us willing instruments of Your healing presence.

Organizing — with Respect

Cleaning up clutter—your own or your children's—isn't easy. And it demands respect for each person's property. But you can organize things if you try:

- Use a laundry basket to collect the messes in various rooms and help you carry them to their real "home."

- Use one or more plastic bins to organize the trunk of your car.

- Clean out those e-mails.

- Reuse old containers—large plastic jars with lids, for example—for birdseed and de-icing "salt" rather than spill-prone bags.

- Keep a paperwork to-do file box and sort pending bills, invitations, and other items into it. Set a schedule to attend to it.

Being respectful and organized isn't always easy. But it's a family saver; a sanity saver, too.

Pay to all what is due them...respect to whom respect is due, honor to whom honor is due. Owe no one anything, except to love one another. (Romans 13:7-8)

Remind parents to respect their children; children to respect their parents, Abba.

Reviving the Bronx River

Before becoming an open sewer in the 19th century, the Bronx River had been home to otters, muskrats, snowy egrets and beavers as well as herring and oysters.

Now Sustainable South Bronx, The Bronx River Alliance, and Lehman College are restoring the river's former natural beauty and wildlife.

They advocate cleaner water, shorelines and stream-side parks. Manmade clamshell reefs offer attractive grounds for oysters. Hundreds of herring have been released into the river. And in 2007, *José* (named for Congressman José Serrano who worked for this project) built his lodge in the Bronx River—the first beaver in 200 years to do so.

Kellie Terry-Sepulveda, a community advocate, says we need to create "a network of opportunities for the community to reclaim the waterfront. It's been monopolized by industry for far too long."

How can you make your city more welcoming to both humans and animals?

There is a river whose streams make glad the city of God. (Psalm 46:4)

Creator, thank You for the glide of wings against the sky; the slap of a beaver's tail on water; the sparkle of silvery fish leaping in air.

Finding Hope While Grieving

Sometimes quitting is the easy thing to do, but it isn't necessarily right. One man from Georgia, Chuck West, learned not to give up despite his grief at losing his son.

After the death of his son Danny, West turned to gardening to create something beautiful and to find peace. But when his cherished Japanese Maple died, he began to lose hope and felt that God wasn't listening, first taking his son, then taking this tree. What else would God take away from him?

But West didn't give up; he replanted the tree and, the next spring, he saw the maple bloom. Somehow, the revival of this tree helped him realize that God had listened to his prayers and had been with him the entire time.

Even if it sometimes feels like God isn't there for you, He is. You are not alone.

For a brief moment I abandoned you...I hid My face from you, but with everlasting love I will have compassion on you, says the Lord, your Redeemer. (Isaiah 54:7,8)

Merciful Savior, abide with me.

Oprah Dreams Big

Oprah Winfrey dreamed of establishing a girls' school in Africa. Now she has made the dream a reality for herself, and others.

The successful businesswoman, philanthropist and television personality faced criticism from some who thought the Oprah Winfrey Leadership Academy for Girls in South Africa was too extravagant. Five years and $40 million in the making, the school is for talented but impoverished African girls aged 12 or 13 years old.

"I understand that many in the school system and out feel that I'm going overboard, and that's fine. This is what I want to do. I wanted to take girls with that "It" quality, and give them an opportunity to make a difference in the world," said Winfrey.

Dream your dreams. Help others dream their own. And don't be swayed by those who don't share your vision.

Education is like a golden ornament, and like a bracelet. (Sirach 21:21)

Inspire many to advance the education of girls and women, Holy Wisdom.

A Sport that Brings Peace

With so much hatred and violence between races, countries and peoples throughout the world, sometimes it's hard to see how there will ever be peace. But one organization encourages children to work—and play—with one another.

Peace Players uses basketball to bring kids between 10 and 14 together to play on the same team. So far, they have brought black and white South Africans and Northern Irish Catholics and Protestants together. More recently they were successful at teaming up Christian and Muslim Palestinians and Israeli Jews even though those groups remain in conflict.

Bringing youngsters together before learned prejudices have hardened makes an immense impact. Perhaps, in time, people from conflicting cultures can join to gradually stop the violence and build respect-filled peace for future generations.

By the tender mercy of our God, the dawn from on high will break upon us, to give light to those who sit in darkness and in the shadow of death, to guide our feet into the way of peace. (Luke 1:78-79)

Jesus, guide our feet into ways of peace with justice and respect.

This Mom Means Business

It took the frustration of a routine task to spark Grace Welch's entrepreneurial spirit.

While struggling to change her toddler's diaper, Welch found it difficult to keep her child from wriggling off the rectangular changing pad she was using. Welch mused, "They need to make a round pad, so it doesn't matter what position the baby is in when changing diapers."

An idea was born, and Welch started by sewing a prototype circular changing pad that featured pockets for holding extra diapers for added convenience.

Welch now sells her product, the Patemm Pad (named for her children Patrick and Emma), online. What started as an observation about changing diapers now generates sales upwards of $700,000 annually. Not bad for a passing idea!

Sometimes, the simplest things garner the greatest rewards. What simple pleasures bring you happiness? A sunny day? A sincere compliment? Someone's smile?

Happy are those who...walk in the law of the Lord...who seek Him with their whole heart. (Psalm 119:1,2)

Enlighten me to the beauty that surrounds me in everyday life, Lord God.

"We're Saving a Lot of Money"

That's what retired pilot and octogenarian Bob Dale says.

For thirty years, Dale and his wife Jean Parker, lived on a 40-acre island with a house that he built. A causeway and one-lane wooden bridge connected it to Woolwich, Maine. The house was environmentally friendly: 150-pound blocks of ice kept food in the sawdust-filled basement cool in summer; there was a wood stove for heat; a composting toilet; a hand-pumped water system; and kerosene lamps before the solar panels.

But, after two medical emergencies, the couple moved to the edge of Brunswick, Maine. Everything they need—doctors, movies, meetings—is in walking distance. They pay utility bills now, but save money by not using a car. They are planning to sell their island to two land trusts so the land can return to its natural state.

How can you lead a greener, cleaner, simpler life? Start today. The Earth you benefit is your God-given home.

The eye of the greedy person is not satisfied with his share; greedy injustice withers the soul. (Sirach 14:9)

In the words of the hymn, inspire our efforts "to come down where we ought to be," Holy Spirit.

Rewarding Family Vacations

Going on a family vacation gives the family an opportunity to spend time together and relax. But consider how helping a community could bring family members closer together and make the vacation that much more rewarding.

A short weekend, or longer trip in the country with a group like the Appalachian Mountain Club can teach a family about conservation while working together and enjoying quality time together hiking or canoeing.

For a more extended trip, a family can visit a U. S. Indian Reservation or a Caribbean or African country and volunteer to help build schools, clinics or orphanages. There are sure to be enjoyable tourist attractions nearby.

Family time is important, and using that time not only to have fun but help people, nature, or animals, makes even better use of that time. Giving is rewarding.

Ascribe to the Lord, O families of the peoples... glory and strength...the glory due His name. (1 Chronicles 16:28,29)

Help parents and their children work together for the good of others, Father-God.

Finding a Quiet Place

Ever feel that your life is so busy that you hardly have any time for quiet reflection? Create a sanctuary for yourself, a place where you can enjoy a few minutes alone. Sharon Hanby-Robie, an interior designer, gives these suggestions for creating such a spot:

- Find a peaceful, comfortable and convenient place;
- Or transform a portion of your bedroom into a special place where you can take "you-time;"
- Fill it with symbolic items, candles for example;
- Do something enjoyable, listen to music or write in a journal in this space;
- As you change, change your place in any way you see fit.

However or wherever you wind down is up to you. But wind down you must, for your health and sanity.

(Jesus) said to them, "Come away to a deserted place all by yourselves and rest a while." (Mark 6:31)

Creator, help me be so comfortable with myself that I can seek out and enjoy time apart, time alone.

The Secret of Failure

Thomas Alva Edison made thousands of unsuccessful attempts to develop the electric light bulb before seeing the light.

Walt Disney was fired by the editor of a newspaper because he had "no good ideas."

Winston Churchill failed the sixth grade.

Ludwig van Beethoven's music teacher told him that as a composer, he was hopeless.

John Creasy, the English novelist who wrote 564 books, was rejected 753 times before he was published.

And the artist James McNeill Whistler failed chemistry, failed at West Point, and failed at engineering before turning his hand to art.

"Failure is how we learn," says Jon Carroll, a columnist with the *San Francisco Chronicle*. "It's not the end of the world. Indeed, with luck, it's the beginning."

So the next time your plans go awry, and nothing you do seems to be good enough, take heart. The secret is realizing what didn't work, and trying a different approach tomorrow.

Human success is in the hand of the Lord. (Sirach 10:5)

Remind me, Lord, that You are with me in joys and sorrows, in successes and failures.

Facing Life's Challenges

Life poses challenges for everyone. Byron Breeze faces his with admirable determination and a positive attitude. With hard work and planning he lives fairly independently though he was born without legs and with incompletely formed arms, each with a finger.

"My magnificent child, he's just what you see," says his mother Patricia Hayes. "He grew up with all sorts of obstacles in life to be an extraordinary, wonderful young man."

Breeze moved to New York where he lives with friends. To remain as independent as possible, he needs to be in good condition. So, he recently trained for a triathlon. "I'm very self-sufficient," Breeze said. "Life is a triathlon. I've got to stay fit in order to do the things I do on a daily basis."

Becoming fit in body, mind and soul "in order to do the things I do on a daily basis" is good advice for all of us.

In a race...only one receives the prize(.) Run in such a way that you may win it. Athletes exercise self-control in all things...to receive a perishable wreath, but we an imperishable one. (1 Corinthians 9:24-25)

Help us attain and maintain fitness of heart and soul, mind and body, Gentle Jesus.

Celebrant of God's People

Archbishop Oscar Romero of El Salvador was murdered on March 24, 1980 because he stood with the poor people of his country against the government's widespread injustice.

He appreciated the importance of each person as a unique individual with a God-given mission. Indeed, he said: "How beautiful will be the day when all the baptized understand that their work, their job is a priestly work. That just as I celebrate Mass at this altar, so each carpenter celebrates Mass at his workbench, and each metal worker, each professional, each doctor with a scalpel, a market woman at her stand is performing a priestly office!

"Cab drivers, listen to this message: You are a priest at the wheel, my friend, if you work with honesty, consecrating that taxi of yours to God, bearing a message of peace and love to the passengers who ride with you."

Let each of us consecrate our work and our lives to God.

Be imitators of God...and live in love, as Christ loved us and gave Himself up for us, a fragrant offering and sacrifice to God. (Ephesians 5:2)

Holy Spirit, remind me that I am a person of worth and potential.

A Special Time For All

Most of us feel birthdays are our special time. But the focus needn't always be on us.

According to the *Pittsburgh Catholic,* Alexa Coughenour asked for financial contributions and canned goods to help the Jubilee Soup Kitchen in Pittsburgh's Uptown neighborhood for her "Sweet 16" birthday. She got the idea from a TV report about a woman who asked that donations be made to a charity in lieu of gifts to her twins.

Coughenour, who had volunteered at the Jubilee Kitchen, "remembered the people there and (that) really made me want to help them." She added "I'm turning 16 and that's a pretty big thing, and I could do something different, to help others."

Coughenour delivered a $300 check to Jubilee Kitchen and that was a "pretty big thing." In fact, choosing to think of others, to share, is always a "pretty big thing."

Train children in the right way. (Proverbs 22:6)

Abba, inspire parents to gently guide their children into whole-souled living. And inspire children to respond.

Have an Average Day

In studying the linguistics of suicide notes for clues to predict and prevent teen suicide, Lyndon Duke found that the enemy of happiness is "the curse of exceptionality." This makes the exceptional few feel isolated, estranged, envied and misunderstood by their unexceptional peers.

Once, when he was himself unhappy , Duke heard a neighbor singing while mowing his lawn and realized that the simple pleasures of an average day were missing from his life.

So when he visited his son at college he said, "I expect you to be a straight C student...to complete your unremarkable academic career, meet an ordinary young woman, and, if you choose to, get married and live a completely average life!" His son did only an average amount of preparation and earned A's!

And that's the paradox of a happy average day: life's meaning comes from the small positive differences we make each day; and from each day's simple pleasures.

I commend enjoyment, for there is nothing better for people...than to eat, and drink, and enjoy themselves, for this will go with them in their toil. (Ecclesiastes 8:15)

Incarnate Wisdom, help us make small differences and enjoy simple pleasures today.

More Than a Tree Grows in Brooklyn

Tevon McNair may live in Red Hook, Brooklyn, New York, but he makes a living as a farm worker.

McNair, along with a few dozen teens in his neighborhood, help run and manage a small urban farm sandwiched between buildings in the predominantly industrial district. He tends to crops, assists in building a green house and gives tours to students part-time.

The farm, which was developed to give teenagers job skills and an understanding of sustainable agriculture, has given local youth a new perspective on life and independence, while making good sense. Says one expert, small-scale farms such as the one McNair helps manage represent an opportunistic and eco-friendly way to better utilize abandoned or neglected land in areas starving for more greenery.

The next time you see a refuse-filled vacant lot, envision a plot of land with possibilities.

The farmer waits for the precious crop from the earth, being patient with it until it receives the early and the late rains. (James 5:7)

May we each learn to respect the earth You have given us, Spirit of Hope.

Considering Compassion

Have you ever considered that compassion is a unique kind of love?

Italian Renaissance writer Giovanni Boccaccio makes compassion the unifying theme of his collection of stories, *The Decameron*. He portrays compassion as the natural inclination "to take pity on people in distress."

Theologian and writer Father Henri Nouwen took another approach to compassion, claiming that it's not very natural to us, and that it's more than mere pity. True to the word's Latin meaning, the choice to show compassion to one is also a choice "to suffer with" one. Says Nouwen, "Compassion is hard because it requires the inner disposition to go with others to the place where they are weak, vulnerable, lonely, and broken."

Although this is precisely the place we most try to avoid, when we decide to enter into it to help another, it becomes a place of profound healing, joy and hope.

If your neighbor cries out to me, I will listen, for I am compassionate. (Exodus 22:27)

Dear Jesus, lead me into compassionate solidarity with those around me.

A Sweet Treat

For many people, ice cream is one of life's simple pleasures. But this sweet treat isn't a new indulgence—whether as ice cream or fruit flavored ices, sorbets and frozen yogurts.

Marco Polo reported that Asians enjoyed fruit-flavored ices. French royalty in the 16th century also indulged in such icy treats. But in the 1700s, when cream was introduced, the dessert became more like the ice cream we know today and much more popular.

Pennsylvania State University offers a week-long ice-cream school for professionals called "Ice Cream Short Course." Most probably, every student does the homework happily.

Keep life in balance. Amid life's trials and tribulations, make time for enjoyment. Whether it's eating ice cream, smelling the roses, or some other delight, treat yourself and others.

If one is mean to himself, to whom will he be generous? (Sirach 14:5)

Help us treat ourselves as well as we treat others, Creator.

Taking Recovery One Step at a Time

Karen Fowler remembers the struggles her brother, Michael, endured after a permanent brain injury. His inability to remember things even in the short term, and at times, his relentless inquiries would try her patience. "After hearing him ask the same question repeatedly, I would be sharp with him," Fowler admits.

Realizing her reaction stemmed from misinformation, Fowler decided to take an active part in her brother's recovery. Together with experts, she began the *10-in-10 Project* to help people with brain-injuries reshape their lives while educating their loved ones.

The results have been extremely encouraging. One person was able to resume his college studies; Michael Fowler became more social and started dating.

Examine your reaction to others' limitations. Stem anger and impatience with information and compassion. Often, those who try our patience most are in greatest need of loving care.

Be patient with all. (1 Thessalonians 5:14)

Dear Lord, infuse me with Your spirit of patience and love, especially for those who suffer quietly.

Stop Road Rage!

If you've ever experienced road rage or been the victim of someone else's wrath, you know how dangerous it can be.

Psychologist Robin Bishop points out that "People are enduring a lot of stresses today, and a lot of times we can't express that. So there's 'displacement' when we're stuck in traffic or somebody takes our parking space."

Follow these tips to keep your annoyance from escalating:

- Don't lose your cool. Try breathing deeply.
- Put yourself in the other driver's shoes and give him or her the benefit of the doubt.
- Don't retaliate or try to get even.
- Reduce stress by listening to music or audio books while driving. Allow extra time for trips.
- Seek help with anger management if you have a problem.

For your sake and that of others on the road, stay calm.

Unjust anger cannot be justified, for anger tips the scale to one's ruin. (Sirach 1:22)

Show me how to control my feelings in stressful moments, Redeemer. Help me rely on You for strength.

A Riddle for You

Do you enjoy riddles? If so, you're part of a tradition going back thousands of years. Phil Cousineau, author of *Riddle Me This,* calls them simply "ingenious questions in search of clever answers." A sample:

"What is the longest and yet the shortest thing in the world,

The swiftest and yet the slowest, the most divisible and the most extended,

The least valued and the most regretted, without which nothing can be done,

Which devours everything, however small, and yet opens the life and spirit

To every object, however great?"

The answer? Time.

It's strange, but true that time can be the "least valued and most regretted" aspect of life. Yet, the more we try to use it for good, the more likely we are to appreciate the time God gives us.

For everything there is a season, and a time for every matter under heaven. (Ecclesiastes 3:1)

Reveal to my mind, my soul, my deepest self, the value of the moments of this life You've given me, Eternal God.

Opening Day

"Opening Day, April 2 (2007), I walked into Yankee Stadium...Everyone...it seemed, rose to their feet" said Bobby Murcer, recounting his experience.

Murcer was a former player and broadcaster for the Yankees. In 2006 he found out that he had a brain tumor that needed immediate surgery; chemotherapy and radiation would follow. During that time, as he had done often throughout his life, Murcer prayed to God—this time for strength, courage and life itself.

More than a million people logged onto a sports website to send him prayers and good wishes. After all he had overcome, walking into the stadium on opening day and receiving a standing ovation, moved him to tears. Murcer, who died in 2008, clearly understood that even as his family and the public rooted for him, God always looked after him.

We are never alone. Reach out. Find support.

I will give you my support. (2 Samuel 3:12)

As You support us, Holy Spirit, remind us to support others.

Fruitcake for Food Pantries

People often waste non-perishable food stored in their cupboards instead of giving it to those who need it.

Throughout the U.S., food pantries wait for donations and are willing to accept those things most people forget they even have.

Another fruitcake? Too many Girl Scout cookies?

Don't wait for the holidays when everyone else is giving. Instead, give throughout the year so that food pantries have food for the working poor and the destitute. Non-perishable food, canned foods, cereal or cookies, sitting on shelves for months are needed every day.

One person's unwanted fruitcake is another person's much-appreciated dessert.

Come, you that are blessed by My Father...for I was hungry and you gave Me food, I was thirsty and you gave Me something to drink. (Matthew 25:34,35)

Inspire us to give generously to food pantries and soup kitchens, Merciful Savior.

Forgiving When Others Cannot Forget

Preaching the word of God, spreading His message of salvation and welcoming sinners into a Christian community can be hugely demanding.

Because of a controversial decision, Roy Ratcliff, a Church of Christ minister, learned that some people would never forgive him for forgiving another. While he had baptized many sinners before, until April 1994 he had never baptized a serial killer.

After killing 17 young men and boys and making the world recoil with his depravity, Jeffry Dahmer expressed remorse and sought mercy through confession and baptism. Rev. Ratcliff says the murderer spoke about being the worst of sinners and believes his repentance was genuine. "He was seeking redemption. He was seeking forgiveness," says Rev. Ratcliff.

It's hard to go against the majority and even against your own doubts. Always ask yourself what Jesus wants you to do.

There will be more rejoicing in heaven over one sinner who repents than over ninety-nine righteous persons who need no repentance. (Luke 15:7)

Give me the strength and the wisdom to do what is truly righteous, no matter the cost, Merciful Father.

Biblical Verses and Our Lives

The Bible is not only a book that's read to us during church services. As Christians we have an obligation to ourselves and to God to read and digest the words of Holy Scripture so that they become our inspiration and companion in joy and sorrow. Here are some suggestions:

- Slowly read a familiar Biblical verse or one that deals with your current situation.
- Write it down line by line with space for your own thoughts.
- Consider researching the verse: its linguistic, historical and theological background.
- Paraphrase the verse and link it to your situation.
- Then, sit, meditate and pray over what you've read and written.

Studying and praying the Bible will help you to stay close to God and to glimpse His very personal love for you.

All Scripture is inspired by God and is useful for teaching, for reproof, for correction, and for training in righteousness, so that everyone who belongs to God may be proficient, equipped for every good work. (2 Timothy 3:16-17)

Remind us, Holy Spirit, that part of being a Christian is to read, mark, learn and digest the words of Holy Scripture.

Prescription for Hope

Gerald Zive first opened his Bronx, New York, pharmacy in 1963, pledging to provide patients with good care.

In 1994, his son Joel joined him, and took the practice a step further—across the ocean to Africa. The younger Zive founded Prescription for Hope, a nonprofit organization behind a specialized AIDs pharmacy in Kigali, Rwanda. Having dealt with tribal warfare and the resulting genocide, the central African nation now battles HIV/ AIDS, a pandemic devastating most of the continent.

No matter their location, father and son feel strongly that the bottom line is the welfare of patients. "As a pharmacist, I have to be aware of not just dispensing drugs," says Joel Zive. "I have to be aware of the big picture."

When you offer help to those around you, make sure that the "big picture" is always filled with God's great love and hope!

The Lord created medicines out of the earth, and the sensible will not despise them. (Sirach 38:4)

Bless all health-care professionals, Lord of Life.

Practical Prayer

What is prayer? In the Bible, it is often portrayed as conversation and fellowship between humans and God. As illustrated in Augustine's passionate *Confessions,* forms of prayer can range from intellectual to emotional. Indeed, in prayer, these two capacities are not separated, but united.

Likewise, writer Jan Johnson resists the conception that prayer is often sentimental. Rather, she says that prayer is practical and moves us to "co-labor with God." While it may move us to tears, it also gives us a heart that identifies with God's compassion for his people.

"To weep with the suffering does not mean, however, that we have a good cry and get on with other things," writes Johnson. "It's more that we have a good cry and we are never the same."

Prayer has a highly transformative element. You should not pray and stay as you were before. To pray is to change.

Lord, teach us to pray. (Luke 11:1)

Jesus, with this prayer, I ask you to change my heart to be more like Yours.

Listening 101

Listening is the greatest gift you can give to God, your loved ones and friends, not to mention co-workers, strangers and, most importantly, your self. And since we can all improve our listening, here are some tips:

- Quiet your turbulent mind's critical judgments, self-doubts, fears and, especially, your response to what you're hearing.
- Hold your tongue lest you send the message that what you have to say is more important than what the speaker says.
- Talk less. Listen. Ask open ended questions.
- If you think your opinion would be helpful, ask if the speaker really wants it. Or, ask what their gut or mind tells them.
- Do not tell your own story thinking to empathize with the speaker. He or she will feel your lack of respect.

Practice listening. Begin by listening to your deepest, truest self.

Sacrifice and offering You do not desire, but You have given me an open ear. (Psalm 40:6)

Help me to be a good listener, Holy Wisdom.

A True Heroine

Between 1940 and 1943 Irena Sendler and 20 helpers smuggled 2,500 Jewish children out of Poland's infamous Warsaw Ghetto. They placed them with Christian families, in convents and in orphanages.

Arrested in 1943 by the Nazis and tortured, she refused to reveal the children's names and locations.

The state of Israel awarded her its "Righteous Among the Nations" award in 1965. In March, 2007, the Polish Senate honored the nonagenarian Sendler, and other members of the Polish Underground, for saving Jews during the Holocaust. The government is also recommending her for the Nobel Peace Prize.

There is no greater gift we can give others— and ourselves—than to resist evil in all its disguises with our mind, soul and body.

Satan has demanded to sift all of you like wheat, but I have prayed for you that your own faith may not fail. (Luke 22:31-32)

Help us hold fast to You and Your Covenant, Yahweh, even in the face of relentless evil. Remind us that our efforts to do good are never in vain.

Sane, Sacred Silence

Our 21st century industry, technology and urban life make it easy to forget that silence exists and is important. Here are a few thoughts:

- "Learn to get in touch with the silence within yourself, and know that everything in life has purpose. There are no mistakes, no coincidences, all events are blessings given to us to learn from."

  —Elizabeth Kubler-Ross

- "We need to find God, and He cannot be found in noise and restlessness. God is the friend of silence. See how nature—trees, flowers, grass—grows in silence; see the stars, the moon and the sun, how they move in silence...we need silence to be able to touch souls."

  —Mother Teresa of Calcutta

- "The deepest feeling always shows itself in silence."　　　—Marianne Moore

These women expressed the truth well: silence is golden.

The Lord was not in the wind...not in the earthquake...not in the fire; (but) after the fire (there was) a sound of sheer silence. When Elijah heard it, he wrapped his face in his mantle and...stood. (1 Kings 19:11,12-13)

Show me how to hear with my heart, see with my mind, feel with my soul, Lord of silence.

Beauty Tips for Everyone

Are you beautiful?

It may be a cliché to say that beauty is more than skin deep, but it's none the less true. The late humorist Sam Levenson offered a wonderful list of hints for bringing out our true beauty:

"For attractive lips—speak words of kindness.

"For lovely eyes—seek out the good in people.

"For a slim figure—share your food with the hungry.

"For beautiful hair—let a child run his fingers through it once a day.

"And, for poise—walk with the knowledge that you never walk alone."

God clearly sees the beauty in each of us. Let's show that same beauty of heart and soul to one another through our attitudes and actions.

Beloved, let us love one another, because love is from God; everyone who loves is born of God and knows God. (1 John 4:7)

Spirit of God, bless me with the vision to see the beauty within my brothers and sisters and myself. Bless me with the desire to grow in beauty in their eyes and, especially, Yours.

With God in Prayer

Do you ever find yourself so worried about doing something the right way that you get frustrated? Maybe you give up on doing it at all.

That can happen not only with mundane matters, but with spiritual ones, including prayer. St. Francis de Sales said something that may help:

"Once you have resolved to follow your affection, don't waste your time during prayer trying to understand exactly what you are doing or how you are praying; for the best prayer is that which keeps us so occupied with God that we don't think about ourselves or about what we are doing."

Staying occupied with God can truly keep us from concentrating too much on our failures and weaknesses. Make prayer an on-going conversation with God, praising and thanking Him, talking over your needs and those of your dear ones. In prayer you will find shelter in God's loving arms.

Father...hallowed be Your Name. Your kingdom come. Your will be done...Give us this day our daily bread. And forgive us our debts as we also have forgiven our debtors...rescue us from the evil one. (Matthew 6:9-10,11-12,13)

Guide me, Blessed Trinity, in my conversations with You.

Animals — Our Best Friends

Animals can be house pets or nuisances. But can they also be just what the doctor ordered?

For Tara Dix, a dog was exactly what she needed. Dix named the 12-pound, 8-week-old Labrador retriever, Dulcinea ("sweet one" in Spanish). Over the next two years, Dulcinea, nicknamed Dulci, helped bring Dix closer to God and others.

Dix found herself staring in wonder at the baby creature, all paws and puppy tummy and learning from her about people, rainstorms, trees, water, television and radio, the world. Dix noticed for example, how, when she sneezed, Dulci would cock her head and try to understand the ridiculous sound.

And, through Dulcinea, Dix rediscovered wonder and soul-deep quiet as well as a frequent invitation to prayer.

Could a pet or nature help you mend your fences with God?...With friends?...With self?

It is good that one should wait quietly for the salvation of the Lord. (Lamentations 3:26)

Lord, teach me to live each moment in quiet and in wonder.

Can I Take That Back...Please?

Without a doubt, e-mail has brought heightened efficiency, speed and accountability to interpersonal communications.

However, e-mail is more than fast; it can become furious when a message is sent mistakenly. Until technology allows otherwise, e-mails, once sent, are generally irrevocable.

Stories of e-mailers who gravely regret hitting the "Send" button abound. A recent law-school grad who reneged on a job offer via e-mail found her impolite retorts in *The Wall Street Journal* and covered in the network news. Another young executive lost his job because of his inappropriate e-mails to co-workers describing his after-work exploits.

Maybe e-mail's dark side is actually a healthy reminder for us all. No matter the mode of communication—think before writing or speaking. Ask yourself, will this message serve as a positive representation of my character? If not, click "Delete!"

A word fitly spoken is like apples of gold in a setting of silver. (Proverbs 25:11)

Help me appreciate the affect my words can have on others, Paraclete.

Defining "Adult"

How would you define an adult? Someone who has passed through puberty? A high school or college graduate? A twenty-something? A married woman or man? Someone who's employed?

Well, here's a multipart definition adapted from *AARP Magazine*. An adult is a person who...

- Knows there are many things more important that herself or himself;
- Is willing to say, "I was wrong;"
- Is attentive to the footprint she or he will leave on the world;
- Forgives the young's carelessness;
- Regrets the thoughtlessness of one's own youth.

Approaching even close to these means identifying your values and then acting on them. That requires prayer, reflection, reading, study—and a sense of humor.

I am the way, and the truth, and the life. No one comes to the Father except through Me. (John 14:6)

Messiah, help us to grow-up and to grow in grace.

The Angels Are with Us

Angels, from the Greek *angelos,* are mentioned in the Hebrew and Christian Scriptures; are central to Islam and known in other faiths. They exist to do God's will and protect us.

Fisherman Roy Pitre was 30 miles out in the Gulf of Mexico with his cousin, Ulysse, dragging for shrimp. While hoisting the nets, Pitre heard a snap. Then his cousin was over him saying, "A shackle knocked you in the head. We've got to get you stitched up." Pitre was covered in blood.

His cousin steered for shore at full speed, hoping to reach a hospital in time. Then they saw a sport-fishing vessel dead in the water. He shouted that they couldn't stop because of Pitre's injury. That's when a passenger identified himself as one of six surgeons on board and told them to come alongside so they could help.

God sends His angels and grace to us in many disguises.

He will command His angels concerning you to guard you in all your ways. On their hands they will bear you up. (Psalm 91:11-12)

Loving Abba, thank You for the ministrations of Your angels in my life.

Inspiring Life

Kate Adamson-Klugman gives inspiring speeches; lobbies for the rights of people with disabilities; has begun a support group for people who have had strokes and helps raise children's disability awareness. In addition, this busy wife and mother makes time to go to the gym.

But, in her thirties, this woman who had planned to become a personal trainer, suffered a brain-stem stroke. Unable to breathe or swallow without help, she "was trapped inside (her) body and given a one-in-a-million chance to survive."

Adamson-Klugman credits God's grace, her husband's support and her pre-stroke fitness for helping her get back on her feet in about 8 months. Still, her left arm and left leg from the knee down remain paralyzed. She says, "I do the best I can with what I've been given."

Do we do the best with the gifts and blessings God has given us?

Trust in the Lord with all your heart. (Proverbs 3:5)

Divine Physician, inspire research into the causes and control of diseases.

Steps to Success

If you've dreamed of being your own boss, you are not alone. According to small-business expert Wilma Goldstein, people crave greater autonomy and are tapping into their passions and skills to get it.

Goldstein has a few suggestions for those who are ready for entrepreneurship.

- Do a personal inventory to ensure you're cut out for self-employment. Most importantly, gauge your passion because "You are more likely to stick with something you love."

- Look before you leap. Research your chosen industry. Learn about applicable licenses, regulations or laws in advance.

- Pay attention to details. Make sure your company's name is not already licensed elsewhere, write a detailed business plan, a simple mission statement and a funding and marketing plan.

Success is 10 percent inspiration and 90 percent perspiration! Persevere, and you'll increase your chances of success.

Human success is in the hand of the Lord. (Sirach 10:5)

Help me avoid pessimism and discouragement, gracious Holy Spirit, so that I may accomplish my Father's will for me.

An Unusual Gesture

The Strait Gate Church in Mamaroneck, New York, changed the tone of the community's race relations by extending an invitation to local immigrants to use its premises as a hiring-site for day laborers. Although it initially aroused debate and resistance, it also spurred reconciliation.

In addition to acting as a hiring site, classes in English, citizenship, on-job safety and nutrition will be offered.

The director of the National Day Laborer Organizing Network, Pablo Alvarado, called the church's outreach "an unusual gesture...a beautiful one, particularly because we know there have been tensions between African-Americans and Latinos in places where they compete against one another for jobs."

Nothing dissolves fear, isolation and anxiety like being welcomed into another's family, neighborhood and life. By extending kindness in simple terms, we can strengthen our communities and our world.

Contribute to the needs of the saints; extend hospitality to strangers. (Romans 12:13)

Lord, as You accept and welcome me into Your abundant life, may I too accept and welcome strangers in my midst.

Having a Quiet Mind

There are some people who maintain their grace and equilibrium no matter how difficult the circumstances.

Robert Louis Stevenson described them this way, "Quiet minds cannot be perplexed or frightened, but go on in fortune or misfortune at their own private pace, like a clock during a thunderstorm."

That's not an easy achievement. Most of us reflect our surroundings and the attitudes and actions of the people around us more than we'd like to admit. Staying calm and focused on what we need to do in any given circumstance, particularly a very trying one, is hard. But it's also the stuff of heroes: not only a firefighter who rescues a baby from a smoky death, but anyone who does a job with integrity and excellence.

Each moment offers an opportunity to practice the self-discipline and courage to reach our goals, to do God's will—if we just recognize and use it.

Search me, O God, and know my heart...and lead me in the way everlasting. (Psalm 139:23,24)

Merciful Father, I pray that You lead me in Your path and guide me in helping those I meet on the way.

Seeing Endless Possibilities

When Joni Owen suffered sudden onset blindness, she was a culinary arts and computer science major. Right then, she decided she wouldn't let her loss of vision stop her from living.

Owen continued her studies, focusing on computer science, and got herself a guide dog whom she named Jelly. Shortly after receiving her master's degree, she was offered a job with AT&T—in Kenya.

In addition to her programming satellites daily for cellular communications, Owen also did volunteer work. She taught Braille to 14 blind students in a local school and helped them get around on their own using canes.

Two girls in particular won her heart. She became close to their families as well. "Their parents wanted to show them that being blind didn't mean being limited," Owen says.

Each of us has limitations. The challenge is to see past them.

The eyes of the blind shall be opened, and the ears of the deaf unstopped; then the lame shall leap like a deer, and the tongue of the speechless sing for joy. (Isaiah 35:5-6)

Open my eyes, Divine Physician, that I may see Your will for me today.

Vexing Problem, Clever Solution

In January, 2008, almost 42 billion plastic bags were used worldwide. But things are changing. In Germany there's a nominal fee for using them. China is banning free plastic bags. New York City requires that businesses which give out plastic bags take them back for recycling. The Whole Foods company is using recycled paper or cloth bags instead of plastic.

And then there's the Republic of Ireland. All plastic bags had to be imported. Rather than outlaw them, in 2002 Ireland began taxing plastic bags at 33 cents per bag at the checkout. There was an informative advertising campaign, too.

Vincent Cobb, president of reusablebags.com, says about cloth shopping bags, "We want it to be seen as something a smart, progressive person would carry."

Earth is your home. Clean up your corner of the earth. Then keep it clean.

Thus says the Lord of hosts...It is I who by My great power and My outstretched arm have made the earth, with the people and animals that are on the earth. (Jeremiah 27:4,5)

Maker of heaven and earth, remind us of our responsibility for the health of the Earth and its creatures, ourselves included.

Bringing Out Their Best

What we say and do affects others. Friends can have an especially positive or negative impact on one another. Michael Angier offers ten ways you can help others see the best that's in them:

- Believe in them especially when they're self-doubting.
- Encourage them, saying, "I know you can do it."
- Expect much, but find the right balance between demanding too little and too much. People can rise to a challenge.
- Tell the truth with compassion and love.
- Be a role model.
- Share yourself, your failures, your experiences.
- Ask challenging questions that will help them think things through.
- Acknowledge them. "Catch" them doing the right thing.
- Spend time with them.

Friendship is life enhancing. Cultivate yours today.

A friend loves at all times, and kinsfolk are born to share adversity. (Proverbs 17:17)

Help friends and relatives bring out the best in each other, Merciful Savior.

A Burger, Fries — and a Low-Cost Loan?

When Steve Bigari's McDonald's franchise began to lose money, he needed a plan. His first impulse was to cut his staff's benefits. His mentor, the late Brent Cameron, set him straight: "You may be able to afford to lose your vacation, but they can't," he reminded him. Bigari got the message. He started to focus instead on helping the working poor.

The plan worked. By arranging day care, providing rides to workers without transportation and offering small, emergency loans and other services, he helped keep his employees on the job and focused on the customers. Employee turnover dropped. Profits improved.

Use your creativity to help the working poor in your own community.

I worked with my own hands to support myself. (Acts 20:34)

Father, remind me that when I work to help people fulfill their obligations to their workplace and their home, I am serving You, the author and head of every family.

Be Generous

Be generous without spending a penny. Here are suggestions from *Body + Soul Magazine:*

- Pray for someone's urgent needs.
- Let go of an old grudge.
- Hold the door for the person behind you.
- Laugh.
- Let your spouse sleep-in while you prepare breakfast.
- Reduce, reuse, recycle.
- Participate in a race or walk to benefit a favorite charity.
- Thank bank tellers and cashiers.
- Give up your train or bus seat.
- Applaud a great performance.
- Give a sincere compliment.

These ideas are similar to that of the old Shaker song that says, "The gift to think of others not to only think of me/And when we hear what others really think and really feel,/Then we'll all live together with a love that is real."

Clothe yourselves with compassion, kindness, humility, meekness, and patience. Bear with one another...forgive each other. (Colossians 3:12-13)

Gracious Redeemer, help me be to be generous.

Horseback Heroine

Fourth graders in one Connecticut school came up with a list of people who made a difference. It includes Dr. Martin Luther King Jr., Susan B. Anthony, Harriet Tubman—and Sybil Ludington.

Sybil Ludington lived in Dutchess County, New York. On the night of April 26, 1777, when she was just 16, word came that British troops were burning Danbury, Connecticut, 25 miles away. Her father, Colonel Henry Ludington, commanded the local militia. So she convinced her dad to let her ride all night through the pouring rain shouting at farmhouse after farmhouse, "The British are burning Danbury—muster at Ludington's."

Those 400 citizen-soldiers couldn't save Danbury. But they fought the Battle of Ridgefield and drove the British to Long Island Sound. Sybil received congratulations for her heroism from family and friends and General George Washington.

Making a difference is simply acting for the good in each moment you can.

Do not neglect to do good. (Hebrews 13:16)

Today, Lord, show me the way to bring Your light and hope to those around me.

Reverencing Life

John Luma's wife asked him to help two baby birds that were stranded in their backyard. Both refused water. One hopped off. Luma scooped up the other. It chirped. Its eyes were alert.

He found an online recipe to feed it. A shaded straw-filled box on a bench became the bird's day-time nest. At night, box and bird moved to a bathroom. Luma forced his "little winged buddy" to hop across the yard to practice flapping its wings. At dusk he brought it inside. Then the bird spent its sixth night alone in the shrubs and Luma knew his job was done.

Luma learned from this experience. He says that "to live more comfortably, we have mercilessly plundered our planet and exploited it at our own peril. Nature, the awesome environment that supports us...needs our care...our commitment to a reverence for all life."

Live your reverence for all life, every day of your life.

God created the heavens and the earth. (Genesis 1:1)

Help us appreciate nature, Creator.

Much More than Stylish

While she was loved by many for her charm and grace, former First Lady Jacqueline Kennedy Onassis was also renowned as a style icon. She was, for many, both a revered figure in American politics and a fashion trendsetter.

While the public's fascination with her style was in itself harmless, it sometimes eclipsed how introspective she really was. The following quote she offered on life's complexity lends a glimpse into her unique perspective:

"I have been through a lot and have suffered a great deal. But, I have had lots of happy moments, as well. Every moment one lives is different from the other. The good, bad, hardship, joy, tragedy, love and happiness are all interwoven into a single, indescribable whole that is called LIFE. You cannot separate the good from the bad, and perhaps, there is no need to do so, either."

What a beautiful way to accept life, on its own terms.

Fear God, and keep His commandments; for that is the whole duty of everyone. (Ecclesiastes 12:13)

Remind me, Father, that true character is built in times of trial and adversity.

"God Planted a Garden in Eden, in the East"

Here are some thought-provoking Biblical facts about the land that was called Babylon, Shinar, or Mesopotamia, but which we now know as Iraq:

- The Garden of Eden is thought to have been there.
- Noah built the ark there.
- Abraham was from Ur of the Chaldeans in southern Iraq.
- Rebekah, Isaac's wife, and Leah and Rachel, Jacob's wives, were from this region.
- Daniel's lion den and the fiery furnace of Shadrach, Meshach and Abednego were in Babylon.
- The Babylonians were responsible for dividing the day into 24 hours of 60 minutes each with each minute lasting 60 seconds.

Every nation should understand and respect its own history and the history of other nations.

A river flows out of Eden...(and) becomes four branches...the name of the third river is Tigris... and the fourth...Euphrates. (Genesis 2:10,14-15)

Just Judge, remind us to respect other nations' contributions to civilization and to pursue peace with justice.

Rain, Rain Go Away

The Christophers always say, "There's nobody like you." Gilbert Center is proof that's true.

The octogenarian is the last umbrella maker and repairman in New York City. He learned the trade in his father's shop where every stitch was made by hand. But, by the 1960's, imports took over the market and most umbrella shops shut their doors. After a brief retirement, Center went to work for the last one, and when it closed, he continued to work out of his home.

There he makes umbrellas for Broadway shows and fixes them for people who don't want to part with their old ones. "They'll do anything to have it fixed, because they can't replace that particular one," says Center. "Maybe it's the pattern, or it was given to them by somebody they loved."

Each one of us is unique and irreplaceable in God's eyes. God never forgets that. Neither should we.

I am the Lord your God, the Holy One of Israel, your Savior....You are precious in My sight, and honored, and I love you. (Isaiah 43:3,4)

Eternal God, remind me when I'm being hard on myself just how much I mean to You.

A Solution for Migrant Laborers

In the 90's, then golf course construction manager Jeffrey West faced a labor shortage.

That's when he began LLS (Latin Labor Solutions) to provide legal entry into the U.S. for Mexican guest workers. Now West has offices in six Mexican cities and a list of 20,000 names.

Migrants deposit $160 into LLS's bank account, and the company completes the visa paperwork; schedules U.S. Consulate interviews; assigns unique bar codes to passports; takes worker photos for the database; and connects them with an employer.

But not just any employer. Wages must be enough to more than pay for travel and living expenses. In fact, 95% of LLS's guest workers are repeat participants.

West says, "It took a long time to find (LLS employees) who took the job...more as a ministry and calling than a career. It helps families and the country."

How can you ensure the dignity of all?

You shall not oppress a resident alien; you know the heart of an alien for you were aliens. (Exodus 23:9)

God, remind us of all who immigrated to the U.S. for a better life.

A Life in Trees

There was a dairy farm a block from Larry Borger's poplar-shaded Brooklyn house and marshland beyond that when his life began over 90 years ago.

A $1,000 settlement from an accident when he was 11 gave him a start at the New York State College of Forestry. From then on, trees have been his life. His trained mind and hands can "read" a tree just by looking at it and feeling it.

Borger has been a climber and pruner for the city parks department; served on the board that developed the Queens Botanical Garden; worked at the tree nursery on Rikers Island; and consulted on landscaping.

He calls trees, "the tallest and largest and oldest creatures on earth." And, he adds, the "secret inner life" of trees makes people feel better.

Cultivate a new tree or an established one. Be tree conscious when buying furniture, flooring, paper or mulch.

**Let the field exult and...the trees of the forest sing for joy before the Lord.
(1 Chronicles 16:32,33)**

Creator, thank You for trees' beauty and usefulness.

Why Do You Tip Like That?

Ever wondered why you tip restaurant waiters, hotel bellhops and cab drivers the way you do?

According to Ann Obringer in the internet article *How Tipping Works,* research shows quality of service isn't always the dominant factor. Often, at least in the United States, we tip out of guilt, not gratitude. She says that "many who have studied the practice have discovered that excellent service only draws a marginally higher tip than average service."

Obringer cites a Cornell University professor as concluding that "countries with more extroverted and neurotic people gave tips to the greatest number...(and) the largest amounts." Outgoing extroverts see tips as a way to get attention. Neurotics are prone to guilt and anxiety.

Whatever your reason for tipping or for any other behavior, it's interesting to consider why you act as you do and what impact you have on others.

Act with justice and righteousness...do no wrong or violence to the alien, the orphan, and the widow. (Jeremiah 22:3)

May our actions agree with Your law of love, Just Judge.

A Gift of Flowers

Flowers hold many significant meanings and are given or used on certain occasions. For example, a bride holds a bouquet on her wedding day, and flowers are thrown on a grave. In these cases, the flowers hold different meanings. But why can't flowers be given 'just because'?

Nan Russell wanted to track down an old teacher and send him flowers as a "thank you" gift, but hesitated. After the tragic death of someone close to her, she feared that perhaps she'd waited too long. Before Russell could start her search, a colleague gave her a bouquet of flowers just for being a good influence. This small gesture touched Russell to the core.

Never wait to thank someone. Whether or not you send flowers, be sure to express your gratitude for kindnesses received.

Consider the lilies...they neither toil nor spin; yet...even Solomon in all his glory was not clothed like one of these. But if God so clothes the grass of the field...how much more will He clothe you. (Luke 12:27-28)

For wildflower-strewn fields and beds of cultivated flowers, for their perfume and their colors, thank You, loving Creator.

Ways to Support Those Who Are Ill

It isn't easy to be sick. We can help friends, relatives or neighbors with a serious illness by making an extra effort to reach out to them and their caregivers. Here are some ideas:

- Call before you visit. Stay alert to signs of fatigue or pain. As a rule, make visits short.
- Sit down so you'll be at eye level. Listen carefully and offer your caring touch.
- Offer practical help to the patient and caregiver, such as running an errand, driving the person who's ill to the doctor, etc.
- Don't criticize the patient's treatment.
- Send notes, cards, cartoons, etc., regularly.
- Above all, always treat the patient as a person, not an illness.

We can support one another in so many ways, large and small. Do your best to help those who are suffering, and the people who are caring for them.

Come, you that are blessed by My Father...for I was sick and you took care of Me. (Matthew 25:34,36)

Divine Physician, show me how to ease the burden of Your suffering.

The Hospital and the Fruit Stand

The crowds outside a Bronx, New York, hospital one summer afternoon had nothing to do with free blood pressure checkups or free flu shots. The buzz was all about fruits and vegetables.

In keeping with its effort to combat obesity and malnutrition in the area, Jacobi Medical Center partnered with Harvest Home Farmers Market to bring fresh and affordable produce to patients, employees and the local community.

"Many of our patients who are used to fast food and can't afford, or even find, good produce now have an onsite opportunity to greatly improve their families' lifestyle," said Dr. Adriana Groisman-Perelstein, a pediatrician and director of the Family Weight Management Program.

A nutritionist is at the market with free pamphlets on healthy eating and even recipes.

Sometimes, improving the quality of life is as simple as getting yourself a bag of fresh string beans, ripe red tomatoes and sweet berries.

God said, "See, I have given you every plant yielding seed that is upon the face of all the earth, and every tree with seed in its fruit; you shall have them for food." (Genesis 1:29)

Nourish us with Your Word, Master. You have the words of eternal life.

Fisherman Catches Attention

When he was six years old, Ted Ames was introduced to the sea by his grandfather, a retired lighthouse keeper. And ever since then, he has studied fish and worked to save fisheries.

In fact, Ames earned a Master's degree in biochemistry and studied spawning, habitat and fishing patterns. In addition, he has chaired regional and statewide fishing organizations. Ames understands why New England fishing got into trouble and is optimistic about a solution.

The MacArthur Foundation noticed. They awarded Ames a $500,000 fellowship (one of their so-called "genius" awards) because, as they put it, he has successfully "fused the roles of fisherman and applied scientist in response to increasing threats to the fishery ecosystem."

If Ames has his way, fishing will survive and thrive — for tomorrow's six year olds and their grandchildren.

Appreciate the wonders of God's creation.

As (Jesus) walked by the Sea of Galilee, He saw...Simon...and Andrew his brother, casting a net into the sea — for they were fishermen. (Matthew 4:18)

Christ, who walked on the waters, keep safe those who go down to the sea in ships.

Cross-Cultural Connections

When Siri Mitchell attended a Christian church in Japan, she quickly realized that "faith has always been embroidered by culture. But we risk creating God in our image when we view him only through the lens of *our* experiences. Our God is too small if we limit him to our culture." Here are some tips on how to broaden your perspective:

- Read international newspapers on the internet.
- Take a personal interest in other cultures.
- Worship at rites other than your own: instead of Latin rite, find Greek, Coptic or Maronite services, for example.
- Vacation somewhere new.
- Enjoy international art and music.
- Read foreign books and watch foreign movies.
- Revise your image of Jesus. A first-century Palestinian Jew, He spoke Aramaic and had olive skin and dark hair and eyes.

Open your eyes and mind to all God's children.

Let those who boast boast in this, that they understand and know Me...the Lord; I act with steadfast love, justice, and righteousness in the earth. (Jeremiah 9:24)

Lord of all nations and peoples, help me connect with and respect those outside my culture and faith.

The Man Behind the Label

He rid breakfast cereal of fatty, highly saturated oils, and is the man behind the nutritional labels on everything edible.

Phil Sokolof may not be a household name, but the multimillionaire from Nebraska has probably done more than anyone—including spending $15 million of his own money—to improve American eating habits.

Sokolof suffered a heart attack in 1965, at age 43. Cholesterol was the culprit, and thus began his campaign to help the public know more about the artery-clogging substance. He organized cholesterol testing for more than 200,000 people in 16 states. He took out full-page ads directed at food manufacturers entitled, "The Poisoning of America." One by one, the food giants started pulling fatty oils from their products. Congress enacted food labeling legislation.

Said one Congressional representative, "He cared, and he was willing to fight for what he believed in."

Our convictions, spurred by caring concern, can nourish the lives of others.

Take care of your health. (Sirach 18:19)

Sustain me, Blessed Trinity, with Your words of wisdom and Your Spirit of right judgment.

Happy Birthday to All!

If you enjoy sending—and receiving—birthday greetings, you'll appreciate the dedication of Antoinette Oberheu's mother.

According to Oberheu, writing in *Guideposts,* from the time her mom Nellie was 16 until her death when she was 98 years old, she sent cards to friends and relatives. Since she and her husband served as missionaries in India, she found herself mailing greetings around the world. Even after Nellie retired, she continued her special greetings. She especially enjoyed telephoning those nearby to sing an upbeat "Happy Birthday"—followed by her wish that they receive "God's richest blessings."

A card or call to celebrate the birthday of those near and dear to you doesn't seem like so much. But, especially for those with few loved ones, it could mean the world. Show your love for the people in your life in ways large and small.

Jesus answered...love the Lord your God with all your heart, and with all your soul, and with all your mind, and with all your strength. ...Love your neighbor as yourself. (Mark 12:29,30,31)

Teach me, Holy Spirit, to use each and every opportunity You offer to express love in every way possible.

"Grief Is Powerful, But So Is God"

Bonnie Woodruff's son Ben, a student at the University of North Carolina, died in a fraternity house fire one Mother's Day. For her, grief was all-encompassing.

The local Fire Chief, Dan Jones, asked her to attend a meeting to get sprinkler systems installed in old buildings like the fraternity house. Woodruff, a former nurse, took the opportunity to speak to the community and convince them of the need for such safety measures, especially in student housing. Now she is an activist working to ensure that buildings have sprinkler systems installed to prevent tragedy.

The loss of a loved one causes terrible grief. But, rather than overpower us, that grief can give us a new mission in life.

Do not give your heart to grief...you do the dead no good, and you injure yourself. (Sirach 38:20, 21)

Merciful Father, help us in our times of grief. Let us find comfort so that we may learn how to help those who are also grieving.

Getting Away from It All

A group of scientists recently ventured into an Indonesian rainforest so remote they had to be dropped in by helicopters.

The researchers from Indonesia, Australia and the United States were accompanied by members of the local Kwerba and Papasena people who had never visited this particular area of the mist-shrouded Foja Mountains. Within a month they were rewarded by the discovery of new plants, frogs and butterflies. They also found a new bird species as well as a giant rat and a pygmy possum.

"It's comforting to know that there is a place on Earth so isolated that it remains the absolute realm of wild nature," said Bruce Beehler, one of the group's leaders.

Yet illegal logging operations are encroaching on even this remote jungle.

It's vital for each of us to take our role as stewards of God's good earth seriously.

God said to Noah and to his sons..."I am establishing My covenant with you and your descendants...and with...the birds, the domestic animals, and every animal of the earth." (Genesis 9:8,9,10)

Remind us that all of creation is bound together in one covenant of life with You, Creator.

Positive Thinkers Needed

Given the abundance of bad news that bombards us each day, it's no wonder book stores are clogged with "self-help" books on positive thinking. Indeed, the times in which we live demand a conscious effort to be optimistic rather than pessimistic.

The good news: you can change the way in which you view the world and increase your energy, too. Motivational coach Jon Gordon makes these suggestions:

- Eat lots of fiber and protein for breakfast and get a day-long energy boost.
- Upon waking, start your day with positive words such as "I love life," and you've started the day positively.
- While on your lunch break, breathe deeply to exhale stress and inhale energy.
- When you're commuting, use the time to meditate, envision a stress-free walk on a beach or even compose a note of appreciation to a loved one.

Hope for good things, for lasting joy and mercy. (Sirach 2:9)

Christ Jesus, infuse us with hope and optimism, every day.

Finding Yesterday at the Car Wash

Ann's nine-year-old daughter Elizabeth seemed only to want to hang out with her friends. Although she knew it was natural for her daughter to grow up, Ann longed for their "girls' afternoon"— Saturdays with shopping trips and nail salon visits.

Then one Saturday, Elizabeth joined her mom on her errands. At the final stop, the car wash, they were greeted with a warm hello from the cashier. "When I met you, you were just a baby," he said to Elizabeth. When her child didn't respond, Ann thought she had forgotten those trips—and their game of singing loudly inside the car as it was covered with soap, water and wax.

As they started through the drive-through car wash, Elizabeth said, "I remember," and began singing at the top of her lungs. Ann joined in.

Yesterday's joys are always with us. We just need to celebrate them when—and where—we find them.

Shout aloud and sing for joy. (Isaiah 12:6)

I sing Your praises, Lord, in gratitude for all Your blessings.

Everyone's a Critic

Do you sometimes feel like you're your own worst critic?

Psychiatrist Dr. Martin Groder thinks that those prone to excessive self-criticism need to recognize that mistakes are part of everyone's life.

He believes that the main role of your inner critic is "to alert you that you're about to do something dangerous, unethical or unwise—or that you have already done something like that. When your inner critic exceeds its responsibility, you experience self-abuse."

"Learn to accept being wrong without suffering," Dr. Groder adds. "Talking back to your inner critic is not necessarily complicated. Just say, 'Stop!'"

Criticism can be either helpful or harmful—whether of ourselves or others. As in so much of life, balance and good judgment make all the difference.

Judge your neighbor's feelings by your own. (Sirach 31:15)

Paraclete, keep me from making my life or the lives of those around me harder than they have to be by being overly critical.

Life Isn't Easy

Everyone complains sometimes about suffering hardships, but most people will never go through what John Bul Dau went through. Born in the Sudan, he is one of the 4,000 Lost Boys of the Sudanese civil war who traveled 1,100 miles to safety from government militia attacks.

Dau survived disease and starvation, and now lives in Syracuse, New York, where he is a hospital security guard and a pre-law student at Syracuse University. With savings from his job, he paid the traditional Dinka dowry, 80 head of cattle, for his wife and brought her here. They now have a daughter. Dau has also brought over his mother and sister.

Dau's ordeal has been made into a documentary. In addition, he has raised almost $200,000 for a medical clinic in his home village. Having survived so much, John Bul Dau knows, "You can't always expect God to make things easy." But, he's happy he can say, "I didn't give up."

Cast your burden on the Lord, and He will sustain you. (Psalm 55:22)

Prince of Peace, encourage warring nations to seek peace and pursue it.

Children: Bystanders to Family Fights

The way parents fight can affect their children more than they realize.

Sharon Fried Buchalter, author of *New Parents Are People, Too,* says that children often don't understand what they're seeing or hearing. "They may think it has something to do with them. They may also feel conflicted, as if they need to intervene. If arguing is a normal occurrence in their home, then children may begin to think that is normal behavior. They may go on to copy that behavior, at home, at school and, possibly, in future relationships," she adds.

Children should never be a captive audience for fights. Avoid threats of divorce or separation which can terrify them. It helps if parents can end by agreeing to some resolution—even if it's to agree to disagree. They should remind themselves of their bond as spouses and parents.

Parents, even in times of conflict, protect your children.

If any of you put a stumbling block before one of these little ones who believe in Me, it would be better for you if...you were drowned. (Matthew 18:6)

Father, help parents protect their children even, if necessary, from themselves.

A Colorful Retirement

George Miranda worked his way up to vice president in the commodities business during the forty years following his move to New York from Cuba in the 60's. But after he retired, Miranda found having so much time on his hands a mixed blessing.

To pass the time and continue his hobby, Miranda painted furniture, one-of-a-kind pieces decorated in rich colors and patterns. He finds inspiration in each object and lets the colors flow. Yolanda Carneiro, one of his regular clients, says, "People are fascinated by his pieces because they are unique."

Just when you think one experience is over, a new one follows. Remember, each day is different, bringing with it new possibilities. So, live your days doing what you love and sharing it with others.

I have filled him with...ability, intelligence, and knowledge...to devise artistic designs, to work in gold, silver, and bronze, in cutting stones...in carving wood, in every kind of craft.
(Exodus 31:3,4-5)

Beauty ever ancient, ever new, help me find the beauty, the inner artist, in everything I do and every day I live.

Walking a Beat for the Needy

Ronald McClosky spent years as a policeman. Now he walks a different beat, volunteering and managing an organization he founded that assists people in need.

McClosky began an outreach ministry in his area after assisting a woman who came to church in search of food. Her needs were immediate, he says, and having coincidentally received a gift of money himself, he felt the answer was too plain to ignore. He gave the woman the money to buy food. Not long afterwards his volunteer network took shape.

McCloskey sees his current role as an outreach minister to the needy as very similar to his former role as a police officer: "I'm just doing what I am called to do—helping others in any way I can."

Any skill, talent or knowledge can be used to serve others. What special abilities do you possess that could help lighten someone else's burden?

Serve one another with whatever gift each of you has received. (1 Peter 4:10)

Teach me the importance of service, Holy Spirit.

Emerging Like a Butterfly

Did you ever wish you could become a new person? For Jana Johnson, this was her outlook at a difficult point in life.

Johnson, a ULCA biology graduate recalls life during her divorce; she had primary custody of their children. She was also part of the Palos Verdes Blue Butterfly project, and had taken a new job 40 miles from home to watch endangered butterflies hatch and to help them mate.

At times, she felt as though she would fail with her children and at the job. But it was in these moments that she turned to God for assistance and courage. It took time and patience, but she was later able to release 4,700 Palos Blue butterflies into nature.

Just as the butterflies changed, Johnson was able to change in every aspect of her life. "They would, like me, be free," she said upon releasing the butterflies.

Cast your burden on the Lord, and He will sustain you. (Psalm 55:22)

Merciful Savior, help me!

Facing Down the Green-Eyed Monster

Jealousy and envy are sad emotions.

Nancy Kennedy told her husband about a book contract a colleague had signed, then complained about her own career. He reminded her that she was an accomplished author of several books and hundreds of articles and asked her what else she wanted.

"More," she answered.

Looking back on the incident later, Kennedy felt terrible. "It gets in God's face and says, 'All that you have graciously provided me is not enough,'" she realized.

When we feel diminished by the possessions, opportunities or successes of others, we blind ourselves to the blessings in our lives. Instead of spending our time and energy comparing ourselves to others, we could be fulfilling our own potential.

As John Wesley said, "To wish to be the person you aren't is to waste the person you are."

Love the Lord your God with all your heart... soul...mind and...strength...love your neighbor as yourself. There is no other commandment greater than these. (Mark 12:30,31)

Beloved Redeemer, help me call to mind the wondrous gifts with which You've blessed my life. Help me grow in gratitude.

Feeding Body and Spirit

For decades Morrone & Sons Italian bakery fed their loyal customers in New York City's East Harlem with tasty breads, rolls and sweets.

"Generations of customers, many of them barely living about the poverty level, often went home to find that Mrs. Morrone had tossed into their bags a lot more bread than they had actually bought," writes Vincent M. Mallozzi in a *New York Times* story about the shop's closing because Rosa Morrone's son Anthony's health no longer allowed him to bake the bread and pastries.

Although feeding others, Rosa Morrone says they were also being fed. Customers, "were like a part of my own family," she said. And so she worried, "Where are they going to get their bread" when the bakery closes?

Her son added, "I know that all of this has broken my mother's heart."

The human touch so often seems to be missing in commerce. How can you share the human touch in your world?

Be merciful, just as your Father is merciful. (Luke 6:36)

Remind us that mercy is an attribute of God Himself which blesses those who give it and those who receive it, Holy Spirit.

More than Cleaning Products in Aisle 3

More and more youngsters are getting high by sniffing aerosol cleaning products, a practice known as huffing. Because these products are easily available and there are misconceptions about it, huffing is common and lethal.

Adolescents are under dangerous illusions that it's just compressed air and it can't hurt you. But inhalants are very harmful and can kill suddenly. Meanwhile, busy, distracted parents are more concerned with alcohol and drugs like marijuana and cocaine than inhalants. However, studies show that at least 4.7 million teenagers have used inhalants at some point.

Parents, take precautions: educate your children early, discuss dangerous drugs and most importantly, talk, but do not scold. Since these chemicals don't show up on standard drug tests be alert for odd smelling breath and a dazed look or slurred speech and empty aerosol containers in odd places.

Protect your children. Above all, love them.

The Lord honors a father above his children, and He confirms a mother's right over her children. (Sirach 3:2)

Father, enlighten parents so they can look after the children You've entrusted to them.

Kudzu Gets the Goats

First introduced in the United States in 1876, kudzu was initially an ornamental vine and then a forage and erosion control crop. It went from being the "miracle vine" to "the vine that ate the South." Growing at an astonishing rate of a foot a day, it smothers flora, swallows houses and blankets the landscape.

That is, until the goats get there!

City officials in Chattanooga, Tennessee, hired a local farmer to graze his herd of goats and clear the east entrance to McCallie Tunnel, which cuts through Missionary Ridge there. Although the solution sparked more than a few chuckles— including "goats working" signs—it proved to "work beautifully," observed one resident who hired the goats to clear a path from her house.

Sometimes the answer to a problem can come from an unlikely source.

In kinship with Wisdom there is immortality... unfailing wealth...understanding, and renown. (Wisdom of Solomon 8:17,18)

I offer You my work this day, Master. Give me the wisdom to give You glory.

I Would Have...

After the humorist Erma Bombeck learned she was terminally ill, she wrote an essay called "If I Had My Life to Live Over." Each line began, "I would have..."

- gone to bed when I was sick;
- talked less and listened more;
- invited friends over to dinner even if the carpet was stained, or the sofa faded;
- taken the time to listen to my grandfather ramble about his youth;
- shared more of the responsibility carried by my husband;
- cried and laughed less while watching television and more while watching life;
- never said, 'Later;'
- said more 'I love you's' and more 'I'm sorry's.'

Life is short. Life's moments are precious. Seize every one. Live every moment.

The Lord created human beings out of earth, and makes them return to it again. He gave them a fixed number of days...filled them with knowledge and understanding.
(Sirach 17:1-2,7)

Remind me, Holy Spirit, to live every moment joyfully, fully, completely.

Scientist Makes Tracks

Dr. Mark Alexander is an epidemiologist concerned about more than facts and figures.

Studies show that one third of American children are overweight and at risk for developing health problems. Moreover, those in minority communities have few resources to assist them. Dr. Alexander decided to do something.

In 2002, Dr. Alexander began a track program at an elementary school in Oakland, California, that didn't even have a track. And on weekends, he and his volunteers taught youngsters better eating habits—and encouraged them to have a positive attitude. The results are impressive. The students are getting in shape, eating healthier and even improving their grades.

Vonncile Harris, a mother of three, says, "Regardless of what is going on in their home or in school or just around them, he brings them in and makes them feel like they are wanted."

You can change someone's life for the better if you try.

Do not neglect to do good. (Hebrews 13:16)

Blessed Trinity, guide me in using my talents to assist others in improving their lives.

When Husband and Wife Pray...

Husbands and wives need to pray for their partners. Here are excerpts from a prayer from Dr. Steve Stephens, author of *20 Surprisingly Simple Rules and Tools for a Great Marriage:*

"Dear God, forgive me for those days that I get so wrapped up in my own agenda that I don't actively, lovingly welcome my spouse home. Help me to make my partner's homecoming the highlight of their day. ...Plant in my heart the desire...to love my spouse unconditionally.

"Teach me how to make our home a haven of joy, peace and faith. Show me how to create a safe harbor and refuge that is close to Your heart— a place where the storms of life will not damage our love...

"Direct me in ways that will make each homecoming special."

Building a loving relationship and a loving home requires the efforts of husband and wife.

As a lily among brambles, so is my love among maidens. As an apple tree among the trees of the wood, so is my beloved among young men. (Song of Solomon 2:2-3)

Holy Spirit, remind couples that they must work together to maintain their love and their relationship.

Building a Global Village

Safia Minney developed a passion for social and environmental awareness and action during her eight years in publishing in London. But how could she cultivate that?

After moving to Tokyo, Japan, she learned to see environmental issues from an Asian viewpoint. She and two university students began preparing leaflets to help locals live more ecologically conscious lives.

Eventually, she started a non-profit organization called Global Village, which has now become part of the International Fair Trade Association. Then, she set up the Fair Trade Company to sell the products of people who are disadvantaged or physically challenged, as well as widows and refugees from Asian, African, and Latin American countries to shops in Japan.

Safia Minney set a great example. There are countless things that you can do right where you are to promote justice and to live an ecologically aware life.

Become an example to all. (1 Thessalonians 1:7)

Inspire business owners to set a good example of honesty and environmental awareness, God.

Contagious Bad Moods?

At one time or another, we've all gotten up on the wrong side of the bed, a euphemism for waking up in a bad mood. But did you know you can "catch" a bad mood from someone else?

Studies show that emotions, like viruses, can be contagious. We can unconsciously mimic the expressions and demeanor of those around us, along with the moods behind them.

Says University of Pennsylvania professor Sigal Barsade, "You can catch a bad mood without even knowing it," making them all the more insidious.

The good news is, good moods are also contagious. Experts have found that in groups where an actor displayed a positive outward expression, participants reacted similarly, reflecting the actor's good mood.

It seems clichés like "Put on a happy face" actually have some validity. Why not try spreading a good mood today?

Jesus said…"all things can be done for the one who believes." (Mark 9:23)

Fortify me with a positive outlook, Christ.

Recognizing Our Treasures

American playwright Thornton Wilder had a knack for stating the truth and packing it with a punch. Like a glass of ice water thrown on us to wake us up, his absurd twist on reality and the way he lays the truth bare has the capacity to provoke.

In Wilder's play *The Skin of Our Teeth,* for example, the Androbus family drifts its way through life in hilarious — and painful — unconsciousness of the truth and the reality that surrounds them.

What does it take for any of us to be more conscious of the truth? Elsewhere, Wilder wrote, "We can only be said to be alive in those moments when our hearts are conscious of our treasures."

Perhaps the gateway to knowing and recognizing the truth is first knowing and recognizing what we cherish. Gratitude, then, glorifies God *and* becomes a sign of awareness and wisdom.

Where your treasure is, there your heart will be also. (Matthew 6:21)

Today, I recognize the treasures You have given me. Because of it, I can live into Your truth, Gracious God.

A Nudge From God

Maeve Smith was looking for a way to serve others. She thought about joining the Peace Corps, but found a description of a Salesian missionary program appealing.

The program was flexible. They "said they wanted people with a sense of humor." She went to Bolivia to teach English, learn Spanish and share faith with the people there.

On returning home she considered a church vocation. Instead, she met her future husband and he introduced her to the Bronx-based LAMP or Lay Apostolic Ministries with the Poor.

As a LAMP missionary, Smith served in a downtown Albany, New York, church. She helps out in their thrift shop and food pantry; conducts a bilingual youth choir and runs a junior youth group, among other duties. Maeve Smith believes that "we have the gift of faith; we just have to share it a little more."

That means all of us. We are all missionaries.

**We are ambassadors for Christ, since God is making His appeal through us.
(2 Corinthians 5:20)**

Help me be Your worthy ambassador, Abba.

Girls Wish to Look like Princesses

Most girls dream of owning that special dress for their senior proms. But for some, that dream never becomes a reality.

St. Fidelis Parish in College Point, New York, though, is doing what it can to help them. It seems that parishioner Donna Finn, who is the principal of Frank Sinatra School of Arts, was told that five seniors were not going to attend the prom because they couldn't afford to buy dresses. Using her own resources, she helped those students.

Then she asked Father Arthur Minichello to put a notice in the parish bulletin. Clean prom dresses and accessories in good condition are now collected for girls who otherwise could not afford them. Father Minichello and Finn are asking local tailors and seamstress to alter the dresses.

Collecting special dresses for a special night is one way to help needy high school girls. How else could you help?

Stretch out your hand to the poor. (Sirach 7:32)

Inspire our efforts to help needy children and teens, Holy Wisdom.

Travel with a Mission

If you have enough time, money and motivation, you might be interested in volunteering on your next vacation.

AARP Magazine notes an increase in the "older Americans who have the passion, adventurous spirit, and life experience to empower indigent communities, and the money to travel to often far-flung places," Judith Reitman writes.

She volunteers at a Romanian orphanage two weeks a year through Global Volunteers. The work is difficult, but it's also rewarding.

One volunteer said, "I feel joyous. I'm part of a continuum of care, a human chain of interaction, touching, caring, and playing. Just think what it would be like if the volunteers were not there."

Another says, "People go because they know they make a difference." She adds, "I though I was going for the children, but I found out I went for me."

God appreciates our gifts of hope and help.

It is well with those who deal generously. (Psalm 112:5)

Jesus, help us offer our time, talents and hearts to our needy sisters and brothers.

Books on Tour

What do book lovers in some of New Mexico's out-of-the-way places do when they want to browse library shelves?

Well, if they can't get to the library then the library will get to them. Many people look forward to visits from librarian Betty Palmer and her bookmobile. The bookmobile is one of four operated by the New Mexico State Library.

A few times a month, Palmer and colleagues from the Cimarron Library take turns driving the library-on-wheels. They stop at school yards, post offices and church parking lots. The readers are always grateful. One says simply, "When you're alone, you read a lot."

What are your community's challenging problems that call for thoughtful solutions?

Get wisdom; get insight. (Proverbs 4:5)

Holy Spirit, give me the courage to face my problems and the wisdom to resolve them creatively.

A Simple Big Day

Your wedding day is a very special, very important day. While planning it, it's easy to forget the most important part—your relationship. Here are a few suggestions from Sharon Hanby-Robie, author of *A Simple Wedding:*

- It's your day, so your loved ones must be clear what you want.

- Keep the reception small and simple. Consider an informal reception at the church or synagogue. This way everyone is happy and you don't have to accommodate too many guests.

- Talk to married couples about how to handle the differences that will inevitably come up over the years. Don't start off your marriage thinking everything will be simple.

It's easy to lose track of what's important, so stay focused and don't get too stressed. God is in charge.

A man leaves his father and his mother and clings to his wife, and they become one flesh. (Genesis 2:24)

Bless engaged and married couples, Creator.

The Gift of Time

"Five minutes: a small price to pay for discovering that only those who are giving of their time have ever owned it in the first place," said Jeffrey Blout after learning a lesson at his local Stop & Shop.

Blout had a tightly timed shopping routine. One day it was different. Blout came upon an elderly couple who delayed him twice while slowly picking out items and blocking the aisles. He became annoyed at them.

At the checkout counter, the elderly couple who were ahead of him on line saw that he had a few items and asked if he wanted to go ahead of them. Blout thanked them, but refused. On arriving home, Blout realized that being in a rush isn't always the best way. Time is precious and should be treasured as such.

Slow down. Live life now.

Every matter has its time and way, although the troubles of mortals lie heavy upon them. (Ecclesiastes 8:6)

God, help us live in the present, neither mulling over the past nor worrying about the future. Remind us that our days and years are in Your care.

A Chaplain for All

A hospital chaplain prays with the sick and their families and loved ones as well as with the hospital staff. That's what the Rev. Margaret Muncie, the only full-time chaplain at Manhattan's St. Luke's-Roosevelt Hospital and one of the first women ordained an Episcopal priest, does now.

But in 1996, doctors removed a benign tumor from her brain. The day after the surgery she had a stroke. Today Rev. Muncie walks with a "lurching limp" thanks to a neurostimulator on her right leg. She says her experience informs her ministry, and adds, "Well doesn't mean perfect. But wholeness and healing can happen, even when there is still brokenness on the outside."

Not one of us is perfect, physically, mentally, spiritually, or emotionally. But we can listen to and pray with and for everyone we know—and those we only hear about.

The Lord ... will not let your foot be moved; He who keeps you will not slumber ... The sun shall not strike you by day, nor the moon by night. The Lord will keep you from all evil; He will keep your life. (Psalm 121:2,3,6-7)

Don't let us be afraid to minister to others out of our brokenness and weakness, Holy God.

Heaven's Doors

Beauty is in the eye of the beholder. And art is one great expression of beauty.

Consider the bronze "Gates of Paradise" panels crafted by Lorenzo Ghiberti for the Baptistry of St. John attached to Florence's Duomo. He created them using the lost wax method in the first half of the 15th century. They depict such Biblical stories as Adam and Eve, Isaac and his sons, and King David.

Writer Thomas J. Craughwell wrote, "Michelangelo gave them their name—the 'Gates of Paradise'—because if heaven ever needed or wanted physical doors, these massive gilt bronze masterpieces would be perfect."

Such beauty was inspired by the Bible. We, too, can be inspired by the Bible to create beauty in our own lives and the lives of others.

The Lord has given skill and understanding to know how to do any work in the construction of the sanctuary. (Exodus 36:1)

Holy Spirit, who daily paints the heavens at morn and evening with awe-inspiring beauty, bless and inspire artists.

The More the Merrier — or Not

Many people pride themselves on being multitaskers, performing several activities at a time. Scientists are not so sure this is wise.

"Multitasking is going to slow you down, increasing the chances of mistakes," says David Meyer, a cognitive scientist at the University of Michigan. "Disruptions and interruptions are a bad deal from the standpoint of our ability to process information."

In one Vanderbilt University study, participants given two simple tasks had a one second delay in responding to the second task. That doesn't seem very important unless you are talking on your cellphone while you're driving your car. Then a second's delay could prove fatal. Neuroscientist Rene Marois says, "We are under the impression that we have this brain that can do more than it often can." He now turns off his cellphone while driving.

Exercise reason—and caution—when you're trying to do more than one thing at a time.

Commit your work to the Lord. (Proverbs 16:3)

Spirit of Counsel, keep me from trying to extend myself too much when I'd be better off taking one thing at a time.

Putting the Wheels of Change in Motion

It was a scene unimaginable just a decade ago: a hundred wooden bicycles clambering across Rwanda's rocky hillsides as cyclists participated in a race—for fun. The riders were neither fleeing danger, nor running for their lives. Instead, they were celebrating a renewed sense of hope.

In 1995, things were different. The country's Karongi Stadium was a place of tragedy and suffering where 800,000 Rwandas were slaughtered in a genocidal war led by the government's armed forces.

Today, Project Rwanda, a U.S.-based nonprofit organization, organizes events like the bike race to raise awareness of the country's past while pointing toward a happier future by attracting investment and tourism.

Even out of the deepest human suffering, hope can emerge. With God, all things are possible.

Hope does not disappoint us. (Romans 5:5)

Alleviate suffering, God of mercy.

Saving a Life

A young woman stopped Heather Fox one day in Memphis and asked for a lift. Fox agreed, but within minutes the stranger pointed a gun and told her to drive to an ATM. When they stopped for a light, Fox fled from the car—and was shot.

Fox screamed, but no one came until 18-year-old Ashley Sanders grabbed Fox, made her lie down, and put pressure on her shoulder wound until paramedics came. Doctors said that Fox would probably have died without Sanders's aid.

Since then, the two women have become friends. Fox even started an educational trust to assist Sanders who's now studying to become a pharmacy technician with the help of a scholarship.

Fox says, "She's like my guardian angel." And Sanders adds, "It's a bond that I don't have with any of my other friends."

A terrible act of violence became a chance for a life saved and a friendship begun.

Seek the Lord and His strength; seek His presence continually. Remember the wonderful works He has done. (Psalm 105:4-5)

Even a crisis can offer us the opportunity for grace. Help us to welcome Your grace always, Redeemer.

Living the Good Neighbor Policy

Thea Rhiannon didn't know what to make of her neighbor, Bill. She thought he looked like a "fifty-something counterculture type from the 1960s," with his scraggly beard and ragged jeans. Rather than focus on his appearance, Rhiannon struck up a friendship that revealed the truly generous and loving spirit beneath his somewhat unconventional exterior.

When an ambulance pulled up to Bill's house one day, Rhiannon learned he had died in his sleep, felled by a heart ailment.

When Rhiannon's then 8-year old daughter lamented that they had not had a chance to say goodbye to their friend and neighbor, Rhiannon explained that the important thing was that they had taken the time to say hello.

Being a good neighbor doesn't mean keeping to oneself and not bothering others. Our neighbors may be in need of a friendly face or helping hand. Reach out and you may stumble upon an opportunity to serve others.

Love your neighbor as yourself. (Mark 12:31)

Help me understand what it really means to love others, Divine Master.

It's Never Too Late—or Too Soon

Kendra Kline was 14 years old when she first heard about the North Country Mission of Hope, a multi-dimensional charity group headquartered in upstate New York.

She was intrigued by the group's work, providing health care, education and community development to Nicaraguan towns and cities. And she enlisted her optometrist father's involvement: "You can be the eye doctor, and I can help you," she prompted.

Since then, Kendra Kline has built houses, painted an orphanage and helped to help purify local water sources. She also served as a translator for some of the mission's doctors. Kline now sees herself going into medicine and continuing to help people through medical mission trips.

Young people have so much to offer. Have you encouraged or inspired a young person lately?

When He was twelve years old, they went up as usual for the festival. ...After three days, they found Him...sitting among the teachers, listening to them and asking them questions. And all... were amazed at His understanding and His answers. (Luke 2:42,46-47)

Jesus, You respect and love little children and tell us to emulate their childlikeness. Protect and inspire them.

Help Along the Way

According to a story in *Apple Seeds,* an Irishman went to see his son off on a ship that would take him to America and a new life.

"Son," he said, "remember the three bones and you'll get along all right."

A stranger heard the comment and asked the father what he'd meant.

"Wouldn't it be the wishbone, the jawbone and the backbone?" the man replied. "It's the wishbone that keeps you going after things. It's the jawbone that helps you find out how to go after them if you're not too proud to ask questions when you don't know something. And it's the backbone that keeps you at it until you get there."

We need to recognize our dreams and to act on them. But we also have to understand that we don't have all the answers. We'll always need others to help us along the way.

The one who enters by the gate is the shepherd of the sheep. ...The sheep hear His voice. He calls His sheep by name and leads them out. ...The sheep follow Him because they know His voice. (John 10:2,3,4)

Christ, I want to follow You wherever You lead me. Help me to recognize Your voice in the people I meet.

The Power of Gratitude

"Gratitude unlocks the fullness of life," says writer Melodie Beattie. "It turns what we have into enough. It turns denial into acceptance, chaos into order, confusion into clarity ... problems into gifts, failures into success, the unexpected into perfect timing, and mistakes into important events. Gratitude makes sense of our past, brings peace for today and creates a vision for tomorrow."

Stephen Post, a bioethics professor at Case Western Reserve University's Medical School, found that:

- 15 minutes a day focusing on what you're grateful for strengthens your body's natural antibodies and speeds healing;
- naturally grateful people are less vulnerable to clinical depression;
- gratitude lowers blood pressure and heart rate;
- gratitude strengthens caregivers in difficulties.

Gratitude is not just a social skill, it's good for you. Be grateful to God, to your self, to others.

With gratitude...sing...to God. ...Do everything in the name of the Lord Jesus, giving thanks to God the Father through Him.
(Colossians 3:16-17)

May my life be a hymn of gratitude, Giver of every good gift.

For God's Children

Staten Islander Stephanie Cimino spent a month in sunny Sicily recently. But not working exclusively on her suntan or visiting historic ruins or vineyards. Instead, she volunteered to teach English to the mostly poor preschoolers at the Waldensian (Evangelical) school in Pachino, Sicily.

In addition to preparing them to learn more English later, Cimino helped the bright children learn songs, numbers, colors and animals' names. In fact, they learned so quickly that they soon sang "What's your name?" to Cimino as she served them lunch. She also helped other teachers wipe noses, tie shoelaces, comfort crying children and serve snacks and lunch.

But it wasn't all work and no play. There was time to worship with the community and for beach time, too.

Next vacation time, think how you can help God's little ones and play, too.

Jesus...said to them, "Let the little children come to Me; do not stop them; for it is to such as these that the kingdom of God belongs. (Mark 10:14)

Bless, guide and protect children, Gentle Jesus, meek and mild.

The Essence of Marriage

> Make husband's breakfast
> Tell him my name
> Encourage use of toilet
> Help with shower...

This excerpt from Susan Luckstone Jaffer's poem *To-Do List for My 37th Wedding Anniversary* captures the meaning of love and loyalty in marriage—even in tough times. Caring, patience, and commitment resonate throughout her poem. Although daily devotion to her ill husband may be difficult, nothing suggests regret.

> ...Cook something soft
> Serve husband dinner
> Say goodnight
> Join "Wolfy" on sofa
> Let "Wolfy" tell me what all dogs know.

Marriage is about loving and caring "in sickness and in health until death do us part."

**Love is strong as death, passion fierce as the grave....Many waters cannot quench love, neither can floods drown it.
(Song of Solomon 8:6,7)**

Author of all loving relationships, strengthen spouses in times of illness, aging or disability.

The "Pop" in Popcorn

Ever wonder exactly how some things work the way they do? Take microwavable popcorn, for example. Convenient, fast and tasty, there's much more going on inside that paper pouch than many might realize.

Three elements enable popcorn to swell to a volume 40 times its original size in a microwave oven in less than three minutes: moisture, starch and the kernel's own hard shell.

When a popcorn kernel heats up, the moisture inside expands. The starchy part of the kernel—the white, fluffy part—also expands, fuses together and solidifies into a three-dimensional substance. As the pressure inside the shell gets high enough, the kernel explodes. The result: a fully popped kernel of popcorn. Who knew that there was so much behind this simple snack?

Life's complexities abound. Revel in every day's and every task's mysteries.

Let your heart keep My commandments; for length of days and years of life and abundant welfare they will give you. (Proverbs 3:1-2)

We praise You, Lord God, for the wondrous world in which we live!

Living with Cancer, Living with Hope

Approximately 10.1 million Americans alive right now have a history of cancer. Some are receiving treatment, some are in remission, and others are considered cured. All of them know that life changes irrevocably when you learn you have cancer.

The National Cancer Institute suggests that people with cancer build a "sense of hope" by looking forward to each day and setting goals. They should plan activities that don't revolve around their illness and avoid giving up things that they love just because they are sick.

Dr. Jerome Groopman, author of *The Anatomy of Hope,* writes, "I see hope as the very heart of healing. For those who have hope, it may help some to live longer, and it will help all to live better."

Everyone, sick or not, needs hope to thrive. Cling to hope.

You who fear the Lord, hope for good things, for lasting joy and mercy. (Sirach 2:9)

Bless me with Your grace-filled mercy, Spirit of Hope.

Plan to Do Good

Most of us like to think that we'll act with kindness toward our neighbors when the opportunity presents itself. But how many people plan ahead?

Patrick Suraci recounts in *The New York Times* the winter evening he was riding a bus on Madison Avenue and an elderly couple got on. They had the fare, but only in bills—not the change or Metrocard they needed. The couple asked if any passengers could make change and a middle aged woman said, "I have quarters."

Later another couple boarded the bus and had the same problem. The same lady made change for the grateful people. When Suraci got up to leave, he couldn't resist asking her why she had so many quarters. She replied, "I go to the bank every day and get a roll of quarters because people always need them on the bus."

How can you help others—even before they ask?

As the body without the spirit is dead, so faith without works is also dead. (James 2:26)

Holy Redeemer, guide my efforts to serve You through the people I meet each day.

Mourning Changes

Gayatree Siddhanta Sarma felt a great sense of loss when her father died. She remembers the flowers her father planted around their house and are now long gone. She writes in *Newsweek,* "In contemplative moments, I mourn those changes." Yet Sarma embraces the future in the same time: she looks to her daughter to cultivate her own garden.

A college student shares a similar ambivalence about past and future, saying, "My own father recently passed away suddenly. Back home, I walked around the perimeter of the house I grew up in, sweet with childhood moments of pancake mornings and afternoon jogs and movie and news nights. Seeing the rooms cleared of his things pains me, but in the pain there is also a great comfort. God gave us memories not to withdraw from and fear the future, but to be equipped to enter into it."

Value yesterday and tomorrow, but especially, today.

O sing to the Lord a new song; sing to the Lord, all the earth. Sing to the Lord, bless His name; tell of His salvation. (Psalm 96:1-2))

Father, thank You for bringing Your love into our lives through the mother and father You give us.

Catcher Son of a Sax Player

As the saxophonist played the national anthem at Dodger Stadium in Los Angeles one evening before the ballgame, his son Russell Martin, Jr., catcher for the Dodgers, was rooting him on.

With every note, the young ballplayer remembered growing up in Canada where his father helped him achieve his dreams. His parents split up when he was only two. So Russell Jr. spent the school term living with his mother, and every other weekend and summers with his dad.

Every penny his father earned as a street musician—who often played in the Montreal subway—went to support his son's quest for a baseball career.

"I guess that when you have two people who believe in the same dream, it's twice as likely to come through," says Russell Jr.

Dreams can come true—with hard work and love.

Has anyone trusted in the Lord and been disappointed? (Sirach 2:9)

Your love is like a symphony, Lord, filling the world with notes of beauty and love.

Golden Generosity

Do you think of yourself as generous? Most people do. After all, generosity implies much more than contributing to a charity, a worthwhile cause or somebody in need. True generosity means giving ourselves, our time, our compassion.

W. Clement Stone, successful businessman, author and philanthropist, was a great believer in optimism and positive thinking. This is what he said about what it means to be generous.

"Generosity is the Golden Rule in action. It is a sign of unselfish emotional maturity manifested by a person's sensitivity to the feelings and reactions of others. Generous persons are kindly, compassionate and experience a nobility of feeling. They have a warmhearted readiness to share time and effort in helping others in a thoughtful manner—and without being asked.

A generous person experiences many of the true riches of life which a selfish person does not enjoy."

Be generous. You will gain more than you can imagine.

**A generous person will be enriched.
(Proverbs 11:25)**

Show me how to imitate You in generosity, Blessed Trinity.

The Quest for a "Poverty Vaccine"

Dr. Peter Hotez spent a quarter of a century researching the hookworm, a disabling parasite which affects 740 million mostly poor people in tropical regions.

Although a team led by Dr. Hotez identified a number of potential sources for a vaccine to prevent hookworm, no pharmaceutical firm showed even a flicker of interest mainly because the potential beneficiaries of the vaccine were too poor to pay for treatment. Deeply discouraged, Hotez considered abandoning his project, but decided to give it one final try.

He applied for a grant from the Bill and Melinda Gates Foundation, which seeks to improve health conditions in the global South. The Gates Foundation gave Hotez grants totaling nearly $40 million to produce and manufacture the vaccine. Clinical trials are now underway in Brazil.

Dr. Peter Hotez didn't give up on the poor. Will you?

I therefore command you, "Open your hand to the poor and needy neighbor in your land." (Deuteronomy 15:11)

Enable me to see solutions instead of problems, Lamb of God.

Use It or Lose It

If you think you're losing it when it comes to your memory, you're not alone.

One reason people say they don't have the phone numbers and addresses of friends, family and colleagues at their fingertips is the proliferation of electronic devices. According to Lisa Anderson, writing in the *Chicago Tribune,* cell phones, Blackberries and other technological innovations provide directories, so you no longer have to memorize contact information.

Whether you know their numbers or not, it's always important to recall people's names. Try these tips:

- When meeting someone, focus on him or her.
- When you hear a person's name, repeat it or ask how to spell it.
- Repeat the person's name when you say good-bye.

Just as you want to be recognized as a unique individual, so do the people you meet. Make the effort to pay attention to others.

The memory of the righteous is a blessing. (Proverbs 10:7)

How can I better acknowledge and respect my neighbor, Loving Father? Open my heart and mind to each person I meet.

Road Trip of a Lifetime

Some students who ride the buses of the Los Angeles Unified School District have a unique school bus driver named Tanya Walters.

She can be strict: "No getting up, no acting up. Period." But Walters also wanted to broaden the students' horizons, so she devised a travel program for them. She took them on weekend field trips and in time she organized the Godparents Youth Organization. Local sponsors helped with funding and other adults acted as chaperones.

In June, 2007, Walters took 22 teens across the U.S. to visit colleges and historical landmarks, but mostly to discover that they have a future. As Walters said, "I get my kids where they need to go. To a new and better path."

Let the youngsters in your life know that they have a future.

I know the plans I have for you, says the Lord, plans for your welfare and not for harm, to give you a future with hope. (Jeremiah 29:11)

God, You have plans for the current and future good of all Your daughters and sons. May all we do and say help us live out Your plans for us.

Future Farmers in the Suburbs?

At one time, the membership ranks of the Future Farmers of American (FFA) were filled with farmers' children.

But as the number of family farms in America dwindles rapidly, so has the number of young people who hope to eventually take over their parents' farms. To keep up with the times, the non-profit, now called the National FFA Organization, has reached out to urban and suburban centers. Today, more members now come from towns, suburbs and city neighborhoods, including Queens, New York, and the South Side of Chicago, than from rural regions.

The appeal? New members, including many minorities, are interested in careers in food science, nutrition, the genetic engineering of food and environmental law.

Whatever stereotypes of farmers may have existed, they certainly have no place today. How can other stereotypes be dispelled?

In passing judgment on another you condemn yourself, because you, the judge, are doing the very same things. (Romans 2:1)

Steer me away from snap judgments, God.

Lesson for Today

What's the most significant thing that you've learned in your life?

The late master pianist Artur Rubinstein described his idea of the single most vital point of human life:

"During my long life, I have learned one lesson: that the most important thing is to realize why one is alive—and I think it is not only to build bridges or tall buildings or make money, but to do something truly important, to do something for humanity. To bring joy, hope, to make life richer for the spirit because you have been alive, that is the most important thing."

Rubinstein was a great musician, but he clearly believed that serving others was the paramount way of enriching our own lives as well. It's really as simple as remembering that in giving we receive.

Like good stewards of the manifold grace of God, serve one another with whatever gift each of you has received. (1 Peter 4:10)

Guide me on the path of generous service, Divine Master. May I rejoice in my neighbors' joys.

Generosity After Imprisonment

Kazuko Kay Nakao of Washington state was among the 120,000 Japanese-Americans imprisoned by the U. S. government for three and a half years in World War II internment camps.

Before that, Nakao's father told them to make "a pile of everything Japanese [they] owned. Then burn them." The only thing that survived was a doll given to Nakao by her grandmother who died in Hiroshima.

Instead of being resentful, after the war her father even sold part of his beloved farm so a school could be built. Nakao remembers him telling her, "This country has given me so much. I came here with nothing. Look forward, not back."

The Sonoji Sakai Intermediate School was named for her father and to honor Japanese immigrants. Nakao donated her doll to the school where it has a place of honor. She now sees it as "a lesson in healing, in forgiveness, in refusing to drink from the cup of bitterness."

You shall have one law for the alien and for the citizen; for I am the Lord your God. (Leviticus 24:22)

Merciful Father, give me strength to do what is right and to forgive those who have wronged me.

Life is Full of Surprises

Charley Wininger, a therapist and dating coach, knew a lot about relationships, human behavior and himself. Or so he thought.

Yet when Shelley Yeffet came into his life, it was quite a surprise. "I kept asking myself, 'How can a woman like this, who is so different, make me so happy?'" said Wininger.

In the beginning, Wininger couldn't believe they were compatible. He is serious and passionate politics and philosophy. Yeffet, a gregarious nurse, has been called "bubbly".

Although they happily dated, Wininger kept analyzing the relationship. "I realized I was in love with her." So the serious analyst decided to stop worrying about it.

The couple, both in their fifties, married.

Isn't it wonderful that life is full of surprises?

Set me as a seal upon your heart, as a seal upon your arm. ...If one offered for love all the wealth of his house, it would be utterly scorned. (Song of Solomon 8:6-7)

Bless engaged and married couples, Lord of love.

Dog-gone Great Therapy!

It's always a happy day for the residents of the Cuyahoga Falls Retirement Community in Ohio when Annabelle comes to visit. Annabelle offers a special kind of fun, comfort and good cheer to the elderly people who welcome her. She is, after all, a trained therapy dog who can relate to their aches and pains.

A victim of puppy mill breeding, the friendly bulldog suffers from hip dysplasia, dry eye and seizures. Annabelle's owner Cindy Vacco has paid hefty medical bills for her care, but is delighted with her dog's ability to work with elderly people. Vacco even pushes Annabelle around in a wheelchair or cart at the retirement community when her hips need a rest.

"She's the dearest thing," says one resident about the canine visitor.

Animals contribute so much to our lives. Let's value them and care for them as fellow creatures who share God's good earth with us.

The wolf shall live with the lamb, the leopard... with the kid, the calf and the lion and the fatling...the cow and the bear...together; and the lion shall eat straw like the ox. (Isaiah 11:6,7)

Thank You for the wonder and beauty of all Creation, Holy Trinity.

Hailing a Garden

For the last few months of 2007, taking a New York City taxi was like sitting in a flower garden — almost.

Hand-painted, adhesive, weatherproof images of giant decorative flowers were applied to cab hoods, trunks and roofs. These images were originally painted by children.

Portraits of Hope organized the effort. That nonprofit group's founders, brothers Ed and Bernie Massey, intended the project as creative therapy for seriously ill and disabled children. They expanded the idea to also embrace those in city schools, after-school programs, and hospitals.

Flowers were chosen because children everywhere draw them, Bernie explained. "It's the one universal symbol of hope, beauty, life, joy, inspiration," he said.

Joy and beauty come from unexpected sources. Find them as you move through your day.

The Lord...will make her wilderness like Eden, her desert like the garden of the Lord; joy and gladness will be found in her, thanksgiving and the voice of song. (Isaiah 51:3)

Slow me down this day, Beauty Ever Ancient, Ever New, that I may not miss the briefest glimpse of Your joy, Your beauty.

Time Treasured

A boy befriended his elderly neighbor and they shared some good times together. But as time went by, the child grew up to be a busy man, leaving his past behind and moving on to "bigger" things.

Years later, he returned to his hometown for the old man's funeral. He noticed that a box was missing from his old friend's home—a gold box that the old man said contained a prized possession. Later, he found that the box had been sent to him. Upon opening it, he saw a beautiful gold pocket watch. On it was engraved the words "Thanks for your time!"

For the elderly man, his most prized possession was the time the young man had spent with him.

In our hectic lives, the one thing we want the most is time. Yet, it may be when we least know it, that our time is most valued.

There is a season, and a time for every matter under heaven: ...a time to weep, and...to laugh... to mourn, and...to dance...to seek, and...to lose. (Ecclesiastes 3:1,4,6)

Father, remind us that our time is in Your keeping.

Love Takes First Prize

As a hobby, Joy and Barry Vissell and their children raise golden retriever puppies which will eventually bring their unconditional love to new families.

Each year this family marches in a July 4th parade, often with their former puppies accompanied by their new owners. Included in this small-town parade are "children on bikes, antique cars, local bands, dancing troupes and seven or eight dog groups," write the Vissells.

Blue ribbons are awarded to the best entries. The Vissells never expect their dogs to win since they compete with well-groomed and costumed pugs, dachshunds and other breeds.

"Our dogs didn't have any of the special things the other groups had. The only thing they had was love and enthusiasm." But that was enough: one year the golden retrievers took first place.

Love and enthusiasm can make all the difference to each and every life God has made. Let's try to remember that.

Love builds up. (1 Corinthians 8:1)

Holy Spirit, help me make love the rule and measure of my life and deeds.

Honesty on a Street Corner

There's a story told about a little boy during the dark days of the American Civil War. The hungry street urchin stood on a corner in Washington, D.C., staring longingly at a pile of oranges on a vendor's cart. Suddenly, a tall stranger stopped, bought an orange from the vendor and handed it to the boy. Then the man went on his way.

As the boy started to devour his orange, a passerby said, "That was President Lincoln. Now, hurry and go thank him."

The youngster ran after the president, shouting, "Thank you, Mr. President!"

Abraham Lincoln turned and smiled, saying, "You're welcome, boy. You wanted to steal that orange, didn't you? But you wouldn't because it wasn't honest. That's the right way. I wish some men and women I know were more like you."

Honesty and integrity are as important to nations as they are to individuals. Strive for an ethical life and society.

Honesty comes home to those who practice it. (Sirach 27:9)

May my thoughts, words and deeds be honest, Spirit of Truth. And may I work for a world of honesty and integrity as well.

Patriots and the Sole Certainty

Being a good American and a real patriot requires courage and wisdom.

Donald W. Shriver, Jr., president of New York's Union Theological Seminary, writing in *America* magazine, says, "We can be proud of much in our history, but we will always need public leaders capable of mixing pride with humility, celebration with repentance. That combination of virtues, I believe, is one we Christians should try to inject into our culture. Isn't Independence Day supposed to be an occasion of rededication to liberty and justice for all? ...

"In 1944 the U.S. Court of Appeals Judge Learned Hand described 'the spirit of liberty' as 'the spirit that is not too sure it is right.' In saying that, he was not far from a Christian vision of a kingdom in which God alone is unambiguously good."

Rededicate yourself to the goal of liberty and justice for all—and to the work of God, the source of all goodness.

The fear of the Lord is the beginning of knowledge; fools despise wisdom and instruction. (Proverbs 1:7)

God, I praise You for your wisdom, and look to You to instruct me. Open me to courage and truth.

All at Home

"To an open house in the evening
Home shall men come...
To the place where God was homeless
And all men are at home."—G.K. Chesterton

One young woman described her aunt's home as not only beautiful, but welcoming. She said, "It's as though you've received a hug the moment you step in."

Our homes on earth are our sanctuaries, places that hold us no matter what. But, the fact is, they change. We put great energy into creating them, but one day rooms occupied by children and parents will be cleared.

At those times ask God to let that "hug" that an earthly home provides become that of His eternal home. The embrace of home, given by God himself, is ever open.

In My Father's house there are many dwelling places. ...I go to prepare a place for you...so that where I am, there you may be also. (John 14:2,3)

Jesus, Savior, thank You for assuring all people of an everlasting home with You.

Buy One, Give One Free

Ever think that shopping for shoes for yourself could help someone less fortunate? Well, thanks to designer Blake Mycoskie, this is possible.

After three weeks volunteer work on a farm in Argentina, Mycoskie was inspired by the simple rope-soled canvas shoe called an *alpargatas* that most people wore there. Returning to the United States, he designed his own version called "Toms."

Moreover, for every pair of shoes sold, he gives a free pair of these sturdy, comfortable shoes to a needy Argentinean child.

This is one way to fulfill the Lord's command to clothe the naked. How can you clothe the naked, feed the hungry, give drink to the thirsty, shelter the homeless, succor the sick, or reach out to prisoners? Ask God for the gift of imagination.

Just as you did it to one of the least of these who are members of My family, you did it to Me. (Matthew 25:40)

Inspire my creativity, Holy Spirit, in addressing the needs of those less fortunate.

Anything You Can Do, I Can Do

The Father Drumgoole-Connelly CYO Summer Day Camp on New York City's Staten Island has two unique counselors. Jessica Mucciarello and Scott Gellerstein have cerebral palsy and were once campers there before becoming counselors.

Mucciarello and Gellerstein lead campers in the Galaxy unit for non-ambulatory children in activities such as basketball, swimming, arts and crafts and dancing. Brian Michael Landano, the camp's director of operations, said, "They don't let the disability make them who they are. They try to rise above it, and in doing so they are very inspirational."

These two remarkable people do not let disabilities hold them back in helping themselves and others.

Encourage all those with challenges to achieve everything they can.

Do not judge by appearances, but judge with right judgment. (John 7:24)

Lord, help us to remember that Your grace is with us no matter what our abilities.

Micro-Gifts Add Up

A San Antonio family that was comfortable, though not wealthy, decided to help their neighbors while staying anonymous. They asked Roberto Piña, with a quarter century of work in church ministry, to be the executive director of their Archangel Foundation.

He's responsible for making one-time gifts of a few hundred to a few thousand dollars that help people in a vast number of ways: a playground at a daycare center; school uniforms and supplies for children whose families can't afford them; payment of a utilities bill for a single mother whose son's medical condition strained their budget; and many more.

When people try to donate to the Archangel Foundation, Piña suggests they start their own micro-philanthropy foundation: "It's a fantastic opportunity for people to grow and embrace the community and understand that there are so many needs out there."

Each of us can do something good today for a neighbor.

The good person brings good things out of a good treasure. (Matthew 12:35)

Open my eyes to new ways in which I can serve You through my neighbors, Divine Master.

A New Take on an Old Tradition

The image of the geisha, women trained to entertain men, is seen as an integral part of Japanese culture.

Today, women are taking their turn at being catered to by men with new women-only butler bars.

As more and more Japanese women struggle to overcome the barriers of sexism, their stress levels—and need for escape—have increased. As a result, "butler bars" have become all the rage for growing numbers of young Japanese professional women who seek individualized attention and a fun way to decompress after a long workday.

Butler bars feature well-trained man-servants who cater to their female clientele. Elegant surroundings create a fantasy atmosphere, where butlers serve food and drink of excellent quality. Tables are booked solid, and even have an 80-minute time limit for guests.

In your own community seek ways to bring equal rights to all of God's people.

Act with justice and righteousness.
(Jeremiah 22:3)

Give Your people a renewed and keen sense of justice, Beloved God.

No Smoking

For many people, the advice to quit smoking is far easier said than done.

Most smokers know that smoking is harmful to the heart and lungs. More than that, "A smoke-free life brings with it much more than just better health; it also brings a better social life," according to Dr. Tedd Mitchell, president of Dallas' Cooper Clinic. He suggests that those who kick the habit can look forward to:

- fewer wrinkles;
- greater appeal to the opposite sex;
- the appearance of greater self-discipline and wisdom.

There is always hope. You can be healthier and happier. If you smoke, make a real effort to stop. If you don't smoke, don't start—and discourage young people, too. Protect your precious God-given life.

There is no wealth better than health of body. (Sirach 30:16)

Merciful Savior, help smokers to quit and enable those who have quit to continue their healing.

Vacation, Now!

Over one-third of American workers do not use their average 12 days vacation. Why? Guilt that they have not done enough or even fear that they'll be fired.

There's a solution to not taking an annual vacation—create a master plan.

- Create a to-do list so you'll know what needs to be done before you take your vacation.
- Tackle that list sequentially rather than wasting time by attempting to multi-task.
- Meet with your associates to discuss work and to share emergency contact information.
- Minimize guilt. If two solid weeks off seems too long, schedule long weekends, say four weekends of four days each.
- Be on the lookout for vacation deals with flexible duration. This can tempt you into vacationing.

Remember: we do not live to work; but work to live.

Six days you shall...do all your work. But the seventh day is a Sabbath to the Lord...you shall not do any work — you, or your son or your daughter. (Deuteronomy 5:13-14)

Remind us to take weekly Sabbaths of complete rest, loving, caring God.

Little Lamb Who Made Thee?

Lambs are regularly trucked to live animal markets in Bronx County, New York.

One July day, a ewe lamb went "on the lam," little hooves clattering on the asphalt, eyes darting as she dodged city traffic, determined to live. The New York Police Department caught her before the traffic did.

Animal rescue experts named her Lucky Lady and sent the ewe to the Farm Sanctuary near Watkins Glen. There her hay-lined isolation stall—she had a virus—is twice the size of the average Manhattan office cubicle. When she's well, she'll join 750 other animals, once destined for dinner, who ramble across 175 acres, living out their lives in peace. Lucky Lady indeed!

Work to ensure healthful living conditions and humane slaughter for animals. Their living and their dying affects our own health, but more than that, it reflects on our humanity.

He will feed His flock like a shepherd; He will gather the lambs in His arms, and carry them in His bosom, and gently lead the mother sheep. (Isaiah 40:11)

Good Shepherd, remind us that people and animals are all part of Your holy creation.

Determination Knows No Barriers

Ashley Sweet had no trouble deciding on the topic of her first novel. Her love of horses inspired her to write *Guardian Angel Dreams,* a story whose lead character nurses an abused horse named Angel back to health.

Sweet did not have much difficulty putting pen to paper, either. She found the writing process "fun," although she considered editing a challenge.

While writing a novel is no easy feat, Sweet's accomplishment takes on special significance when one considers that she was just 11 years old when she began planning and writing her book, which was published when the author was just 13. She's now writing a sequel.

Every individual has something worthwhile to contribute to the world. Young people can make a difference in a multitude of ways. Offer them your encouragement.

Let us work for the good of all. (Galatians 6:10)

Son of God, offer Your gracious protection to all Your children — and ours.

The Ripple Effect

New Orleans octogenarian Clarence Barbour had already experienced a great deal in his long life before Hurricane Katrina.

After Katrina's devastation, Barbour and his wife, Emma Jean, were evacuated to a relief center in Waldron, Arkansas. They decided to remain there.

In an article for the *Glenmary Challenge,* lay missioner Kathy O'Brien wrote about the Barbours and several other people who were candidates for baptism into the Catholic Church. Although different circumstances had influenced each of them, all decided to convert based on positive relationships with others.

The Barbours, for example, became involved with parish life at St. Jude Thaddeus Church in Waldron. Parishioners had helped them move from New Orleans. Clarence Barbour said, "If a person is friend enough to move you and is not trying to sell you anything, I was impressed by that kind of generosity and care."

Disinterested deeds of loving kindness are indeed powerful.

Just as I have loved you, you also should love one another. (John 13:34)

May love be my rule of life, Loving Jesus.

Thou Shalt Love Thy Spouse

Happy marriages take love and perseverance from both husband and wife. Gregory Godek, author of *10,000 Ways to Say I Love You*, offers his thoughts on 10 Commandments of Marriage:

1. Thou shalt be committed to thy union.
2. Thou shalt treat your partner as your equal.
3. Thou shalt pepper your communications with courtesy.
4. Thou shalt respect and learn from your differences.
5. Thou shalt act lovingly toward one another.
6. Thou shalt work toward common goals.
7. Thou shalt communicate openly and honestly.
8. Thou shalt be friends as well as lovers.
9. Thou shalt not be mean to one another.
10. Thou shalt let your love for each other take priority over all other priorities.

Give your spouse tender, loving care each and every day of your lifetime together.

If I...do not have love, I am a noisy gong or a clanging cymbal. ...If I have all faith...but do not have love, I am nothing. (1 Corinthians 13:1,2)

Bless all married couples, God of love. Help them live and love in Your love.

Sew Much Care

If you've ever tried to put on clothes while wearing a cast, you know it's not easy. Now think about returning U.S. service men and women who face weeks or months of rehabilitation with casts, prosthetic limbs or other conditions which impede their ability to put on and wear regular clothing.

That's where Sew Much Comfort steps in. Since 2004, the volunteers have adapted tee shirts, pants, shorts, underwear, swimwear used for therapy, and more. Velcro, snaps, etc., allow patients to dress themselves in something more comfortable and attractive than hospital gowns. More than 30,000 articles of clothing have been made and distributed to U. S. service members at home and around the world.

Each piece of clothing offers not only a sense of normalcy, but also tangible proof of the volunteers' concern for military personnel injured in the line of duty.

Opportunities to aid others abound. We only have to look for them.

Do not hesitate to visit the sick. (Sirach 7:35)

Holy Redeemer, thank You for guiding us in showing our love for our brothers and sisters.

Can Business and Spirituality Mix?

Jose Zeilstra grew up in a church which concentrated on sending members overseas to share the gospel. "The feeling was if you're a true Christian, you enter the ministry; the business world wasn't a place for believers," she says. When Zeilstra began moving up through the ranks at her corporate job, the conflict seemed to peak for her.

Then she read *Roaring Lambs* by Bob Briner, a book that says that Christians should be a beacon of light in all areas of life. Zeilstra realized that her career was a legitimate calling from God.

Rather than keep her faith private, she started to express her beliefs. "The first time I spoke publicly about my faith was for *Fortune* magazine," she says. "In the business world, it doesn't get more public than that." Zeilstra also speaks at Bible study groups for other corporate professionals.

Being "a beacon of light" means not just discussing but living out one's faith moment by moment.

You are the salt of earth...You are the light of the world. (Matthew 5:13,14)

Remind us, Carpenter from Nazareth, that it's on Your good earth that we are to live out the Father's law of love.

Dear Mr. Rogers

The late Fred Rogers was not only much beloved by the children who tuned into TV's *Mr. Rogers' Neighborhood,* but by the adults they grew up to be. One of his favorite quotes was Antoine de Sainte-Exupéry's idea that "What is essential is invisible to the eye." Rogers clearly saw the essence of others.

Tim Madigan found that to be true. Suffering from depression, he turned to Rogers—a man he's only met once and with whom he had a slight correspondence—to ask advice.

Madigan poured his heart into a letter, finally asking: "Will you be proud of me?" Rogers responded: YES, "I will be proud of you. I am proud of you."

Madigan took that letter and those that followed as "an affirmation of [his] worth as a person."

Sometimes a kind word can turn someone's life around.

Kindness is like a garden of blessings. (Sirach 40:17)

Divine Lord, help me never to forget that something as simple as a heart-felt letter is a way of reaching out.

Leaving the Fast Lane

If you find yourself needing to slow down to appreciate the moment, Chrystle Fiedler offers these tips in *Woman's Day:*

- Ditch the list mindset. "List consciousness operates on the premise that life will happen once everything is crossed off your to-do list," notes therapist Abby Seixas. "You're not focusing on what you're doing now, you're focusing on what you have to do next. In the process you miss out on your life."

- Decompress between tasks. For example, the next time you return a library book, take time to browse the shelves.

- Really listen. In conversation, don't be judgmental or distracted; don't just wait for your turn to speak. Hear the other person.

- Build slow rituals into your day. Share a cup of tea. Hold the door for someone.

Savor that journey which is your life.

The race is not to the swift, nor the battle to the strong, nor bread to the wise, nor riches to the intelligent, nor favor to the skillful; but time and chance happen to them all. (Ecclesiastes 9:11)

Remind me, Merciful Savior, to slow down and enjoy the life You've given me.

Troubled Waters

Lynne Cox has swum the English Channel and the seven seas and what she's learned is that "the biggest danger in the ocean isn't always sharks. More often than not, man-made hazards pose the greatest threat."

During a swim off California, Cox, who has several long distance swimming records, rescued a pelican tangled in a fishing line with three hooks embedded in its feathers. The pollution around her included garbage bags that choke seals who mistake them for fish. But "the worst was swimming the Nile in '74. It smelled like a sewer" and her "fingers were cut by broken glass."

As she swims and feels the movement of the creatures around her, it reminds her that she's "a guest in the beautiful home God gave them" and that "the earth does not belong to us. It belongs to Heaven."

The earth and its waters are both a gift and a responsibility.

God said, "Let the waters bring forth swarms of living creatures"...the great sea monsters and every living creature...God saw that it was good. God blessed them saying, "...fill the waters in the seas." (Genesis 1:20,21,22)

Creator, help me to respect nature and to remember that like nature I am but Your creation.

"Food Is Love"

In 2003, Jayne Steiner-Kanak's mother was terminally ill, so Steiner-Kanak took a leave of absence to be with her. She helped her mother through her rigorous daily routine, always trying to add fun activities whenever possible.

Then, it occurred to her: food and cooking had been a big part of her mom's life. So, although the holidays were a few months off, why not celebrate them early?

Steiner-Kanak's family and friends loved the idea and immediately pitched in. First, they celebrated Thanksgiving and then set the stage for a summer Christmas, tree and all. Despite her failing health, her mom greatly enjoyed these celebrations.

On her mother's death just weeks later, Steiner-Kanak remembered her words, "Food is love."

Food is indeed one way to express love. But remember that genuine love can only be freely given and freely accepted.

Let love be genuine. ...Love one another with mutual affection. (Romans 12:9, 10)

Remind parents that genuine love is a free gift, Loving Jesus.

Listening — the Ultimate Skill

Walter Hood is a professor of landscape architecture at the University of California, Berkeley. He is also a public advocate and pioneer who's known for his ability and willingness to listen.

Before Hood redesigns a local park, he spends a lot of time observing, talking with and listening to neighborhood residents. He says, "People respond to the familiar. So we want to take the familiar and heighten it."

He seeks to understand the history of a place by observing it over time and listening to community needs. Hood adds, "I'm interested in how the everyday mundane practices of life get played out in cities, the unheralded patterns that take place without celebration. There's a structure to cities, a 4/4 beat. Designing is like improvisation, finding a sound for each place."

Listening is key to understanding and improvisation. Learn to be an attentive and active listener.

Pay attention to how you listen. (Luke 8:18)

Open not just my ears, but my mind, heart, soul, even my body to listen with every fiber of my being, Holy Wisdom.

A Heart for Others

When Amy Berman of Minneapolis read about the two million children in Africa with AIDS in 2003, she decided she had to reach out to them.

Her mother had given knitted bears to Berman's children which had offered them great comfort. So Berman asked her mom for a refresher course in knitting and got started. Each bear is unique, but each features an appliquéd felt heart. Soon the idea spread to other knitters and now the Mother Bear Project has sent 14,000 bears to African children.

One boy said that he especially treasures the bear because the heart "means that someone loves him."

Do something today to comfort a child, particularly one who could really benefit from your personal attention and tender loving care.

Is there anyone among you who, if your child asks for bread, will give a stone? Of if the child asks for a fish, will give a snake? If you then... give good gifts to your children, how much more will your Father...give good things to those who ask Him! (Matthew 7:9-11)

Merciful Father, show me how to share the gifts You've offered me with those in need.

Environmental Wakeup

How many times have you heard the issue of recycling come up? Or have you wondered how the rainforest is doing?

One company takes both recycling and the rainforest into consideration. TerraCycle makes eco-friendly plant food packaged in recycled soda bottles. The company is the idea of two Princeton University students, Tom Szaky and Jon Beyer, who began with the idea of taking waste from the campus and processing it into a useful product. Szaky and Beyer have since created bottle, yogurt, and drink pouch brigades to collect the material.

According to Nicole Lorimer, a writer for *Guideposts,* "The Bottle Brigade has rescued 1.8 million bottles from ending up in landfills and saved 22,000 square feet of rainforest."

It only takes one idea and the courage to expand on it to help save our environment.

The Lord...formed the earth and made it (...He did not create it a chaos, He formed it to be inhabited!) (Isaiah 45:18)

Creator, help us walk lightly upon Your earth, our home.

About Sobriety

Becoming sober is a big step for addicts. Laura M. dreaded going home for a visit in light of her alcoholic addiction. Instead, she attended an Alcoholics Anonymous meeting.

Laura M. would often sink into deep depressions and think dark thoughts. That all changed for her after a woman spoke about her own similar problems and said that she was working through it. Finally, Laura M. understood that others were experiencing the same challenges that she was.

After the meeting, she thought, "Okay, God, now I get it. I understand why all these people are here and I understand why I'm here too. Thank you."

Sobriety is a path no one can walk alone. People who can best understand and offer support are those who have themselves emerged from the experience.

Christ, will Himself restore, support, strengthen, and establish you. (1 Peter 5:10)

Teach me to lean on You; remind me to lean on You; help me to lean on You—merciful Jesus.

Old Tractors

Kyle Kramer, a Midwestern farmer, admits that his farming equipment is a rusty eyesore. But he's committed to caring for his old machines, monitoring their fluids and replacing broken parts. The less urgent repairs wait.

Kramer, writing in *America* magazine, does not hide behind a guise of practicality, however. He believes that we can't hide from signs of decline. Rather, keeping old tractors is partly symbolic. "Do we pledge fidelity to the old things—and old people—that have given us much over a long life?" he asks. "Do we honor these long lives and accompany them to the scrap heap or the grave with thanksgiving and gentleness? Do we show a little mercy and tender affection in the hope that as we age others might show us the same?"

This farmer knows that loyalty and affection for things and, especially, people, is a timeless practice.

I will take you for my wife forever; I will take you for my wife in righteousness and in justice, in steadfast love, and in mercy. (Hosea 2:19)

Dear Lord, help me show loyalty to all the men and women who have given me much during my life—and theirs.

Dreams of Space for All

When a little girl told Becca Robison, then only 10, that she couldn't be an astronaut because it was a "boy's job," she didn't get discouraged.

The Utah native, now a teen, whose love for science began when her older brother taught her about constellations, decided to create a special camp. She called it Astro Tots Science Camp for Little Dippers and held day-long workshops in her backyard to teach other girls about planets and technology.

When word of the project spread, Becca Robison was asked to hold camps in local parks and community centers. She even received a presidential honor for her efforts.

One of the campers put it this way: "Becca teaches you stuff you never knew before and inspires you."

Don't give up your dreams. Your ambitions could inspire others.

Encourage one another. (1 Thessalonians 5:11)

Protect, bless, and encourage all who want to pursue non-traditional goals.

For Better Health

Good health is a gift and a treasure. That means you have to play an active role in its preservation. Here are some suggestions from Dr. Andrew Weil:

- Go to sleep 10 minutes earlier so you can awaken 10 minutes earlier and enjoy the stillness and solitude.
- Seek tranquility to sooth your nerves and stress-addled brain.
- After that first cup of coffee, substitute tea or decaffeinated coffee.
- Make an effort to eat slowly, mindfully, so you can savor the taste of the food and be satisfied with less of it.
- Try not to sit for long periods.
- If only for a minute a day, take slow, deep breaths to ease stress.
- Add fresh fruit to each breakfast.

Do all you can to be healthier, less frenetic, and quieter. After all, it's your health.

There is...no gladness above joy of heart. (Sirach 30:16)

Divine Physician, inspire my moment-by-moment efforts to live more healthfully.

Mother to the Mustangs

Karen Sussman has named virtually every one of the 350 horses on her 680-acre ranch near Lantry, South Dakota.

The 60-year-old registered nurse has spent the past 20 years as the head of the International Society for the Protection of Mustangs and Burros, an organization begun to save wild horses in the United States from elimination and slaughter.

Caring for the horses can be costly. To defray those expenses, Sussman provides close-up tours of the horses in their prairie pastures. Donors can sponsor a horse, an orphaned foal, a band or an entire herd.

"It's just a phenomenal sight to be able to watch these horses," she says.

God made the earth and all creatures, asking us to nurture and care for them with wisdom.

Do you give the horse its might?...clothe its neck with mane?...make it leap like the locust? Its majestic snorting is terrible. It paws violently, exults mightily. (Job 39:19,20-21)

Creator, thank You for horses' powerful, graceful beauty. Send Your Spirit to guide us as we safeguard them and all animals.

A Life of Befriending

Befriending others was Reverend David Kirk's passion. When he was a teen, he got permission to enroll in a black high school for a month to share, to some extent, the experiences of those who faced the inequalities of the Jim Crow Laws. He said that this prepared him for a life of service.

After college and his ordination, Reverend Kirk went to Alabama to join the Civil Rights Movement. Next, he went to New York to found and run a homeless shelter. He called it Emmaus House, after the road on which Jesus was first seen by his disciples after his resurrection. The House became his life project, the place where he lived along with 14 homeless men.

Even as his health deteriorated and his kidneys failed, he declined their offers to donate, saying, "I couldn't take something they need so much." Here was a man who gave all he had in the service of God's people.

Remember those who are in prison, as though you were in prison with them; those who are being tortured, as though you yourselves were being tortured. (Hebrews 13:3)

Dear Jesus, may I, along with Your disciples, know what it is to see and to follow You on the Emmaus Road.

Once in a Lifetime

Opportunity…every one of us looks for it, but it flies by us more often than we realize. How often do we make the most of it? Jason McElwain is one who did.

McElwain, an autistic New York teen, captured the imagination of the nation in just five minutes. An avid basketball fan, he never got to play for his school team in Rochester, New York, until his coach put him in for the final five minutes of the last game of his last season. In those moments, he scored 20 points and led his team to victory.

Jason was given an opportunity, grabbed it, and created a moment to cherish.

When a once in a lifetime opportunity comes your way, pray for the wisdom to recognize it and the courage to take hold of it with both hands.

God of my ancestors and Lord of mercy, who… by Your wisdom have formed humankind to… rule the world in holiness and righteousness… give me the wisdom that sits by Your throne. (Wisdom of Solomon 9:1,2,3,4)

Creator, I want to be all that You created me to be. Aid me.

Is Your Soul Hungry?

Most of us have no trouble remembering to eat in order to stave off physical hunger. But more and more of us are forgetting to feed our souls.

Growing numbers of Americans are admitting that they are starved for personal time, for the opportunity to get in touch with themselves and to feed their souls with enjoyable, fulfilling pursuits—or with doing nothing.

One therapist suggests that you identify what you love to do, including activities that speak to your soul's passions. Try to engage in even one of them each month. And, schedule leisure and a little room for fun—first.

Psychologist Kenneth W. Christian believes that you should "cocoon yourself in silence" at least once a day. Silence the noise of electronic devices, like car radios, TVs and computers.

Feed your soul with time, attention and silence.

Seek the Lord and His strength, seek His presence continually. (1 Chronicles 16:11)

Give me the wisdom and courage to slow down and enter into silence, Father, so that my soul may thrive.

Second Hand, First Class

Danielle Butin, a managed care executive, knew that hospitals often had items that they could not use. For example, shrink-wrapped supplies were thrown away after every surgery; the same for still-sterile sutures after the outer plastic wrap had come off; surgical gloves, sponges, tape, etc. were also wasted. Meanwhile, doctors in other countries lack these supplies.

After she was laid off and had time, Butin asked a Haitian hospital to send her its "shopping list." Inventory controllers at various hospitals were delighted when she volunteered to take usable medical supplies off their hands. Soon the first 40-foot container was headed to Haiti.

Now she's begun the non-profit Afya (Swahili for health) Foundation of America. Butin has a warehouse and overseas hospitals are eager for her help.

What can you do to bring the basics to those who lack even these both at home and abroad?

It is a question of a fair balance between your present abundance and their need. (2 Corinthians 8:13)

Help us to share rather than waste our abundance, God.

Disabilities — or Different Abilities?

Most dogs can understand just a few words such as sit and stay. But Hogan, a 13-year-old Dalmatian, understands more than 60 American Sign Language commands.

Hogan was born deaf and was abused until he was rescued by an owner willing to learn American Sign Language herself and then teach it to him.

Over time, Hogan has become famous in his home of Killingworth, Connecticut, and beyond. He's appeared on television, and college students visit him to learn his story and see him in action. The dog is part of an effort to change the way people think about deafness in animals.

Because Hogan had a disability—and because he was cared for and loved—his special ability was discovered.

There's a lesson in that for us all.

Do not judge by appearances. (John 7:24)

Never let us forget, Blessed Creator, that all life is precious and that genuine perfection is Yours alone.

Seeking Genuine Rest

"What if genuine living and genuine rest are intimately intertwined?" This is writer Jennifer Louden's question.

Have you ever returned from a lunch break and found yourself exhausted? Such a statement seems contradictory: exhausted after a break? But the late writer Father Henri Nouwen pointed out a similar irony, that one returning from a party may feel lonelier than one did before going.

In rest and renewal, God calls us back to Him, yet, too often we see rest as a disruption to accomplishing all we want to do.

Rest is powerful if we acknowledge it for what God created it to be: a remembrance of Him. He gives us space to realize and to confirm our genuine selves, and the resources to be creative. In Him we find both genuine living and genuine rest.

Return, O my soul, to your rest, for the Lord has dealt bountifully with you. For You have delivered my soul from death, my eyes from tears, my feet from stumbling. (Psalm 116:7-8)

Dear Redeemer, help me see that I need to turn to You for rest, for You bring me home and make my tired heart glad.

Catching a Fish and a Break

"Fishing lets you forget all your troubles, at least for a little while," believes Andy Powers.

So, when he heard that a group in New Jersey organized a "Take a Vet Fishing Day" as a way of offering support—and some fun—to veterans who've served the United States, he decided to do the same. He fixed up his boat and placed an ad in a local paper offering outings and encouraging others to take vets and active-duty military men and women fishing.

Powers even started a website to get more commercial and recreational fishermen involved. As Anthony Reina of Point Pleasant, New Jersey, who runs a charter fishing fleet, says, "I'm enlisted in the Coast Guard reserves, so I understand the pressures. This is the least I can do."

We owe a debt of gratitude to so many people. Let's express our appreciation every chance we get.

If you do good, know to whom you do it, and you will be thanked for your good deeds. Do good to the devout, and you will be repaid — if not by them, certainly by the Most High. (Sirach 12:1-2)

Remind me, Holy Spirit, to say "thank you" to my brothers and sisters to whom I owe so much.

Boxed In

Those minutes each morning spent reaching your office floor via elevator can be uncomfortable. Not knowing what to say to people you barely know, you stare at your watch, glance at some papers, or look up at lit numbers. But elevator rides don't have to be so awkward if you "keep the small talk concise and banal."

According to conversation expert Don Gabor, "trite is right and cliché is OK." The latest news, sports scores or weather report is perfect for such a situation. "You don't have to be brilliant. You just have to be nice."

So next time you find yourself in the elevator corner fifteen floors away from your stop, just smile to the person next to you and make a comment about how "the 'three month' renovation of your building is now in its fourth year." Chances are you'll both feel better about starting the day.

Pleasant words are like a honeycomb, sweetness to the soul and health to the body. (Proverbs 16:24)

Heavenly Father, help me make another person's day brighter with a simple 'good morning' or a welcoming smile.

Protecting Africa's Precious Resources

In 2006, an innovative plan set the stage for environmental protection in Africa. France and Cameroon signed a debt-for-nature swap that aims to conserve some of the most pristine and threatened rainforest in Africa.

Under the agreement, at least $25 million will be invested over five years to protect parts of the Congo River Basin, the world's second largest tropical forest after the Amazon. In addition, the fund will be used to reduce poverty through its debt-relief strategy.

When you start focusing on solutions, not problems, a world of change can open up.

When the poor and needy seek water...I the Lord...will open rivers on the bare heights, and fountains in the midst of the valleys; I will make the wilderness a pool of water, and the dry land springs of water. (Isaiah 41:17,18)

Gracious God, inspire us to protect the life-sustaining rivers and springs You've given us and earth's creatures.

A Man of Conscience

The word "martyr" might make you think of early Christians slaughtered in the Roman coliseum, but every century has seen people killed for their beliefs. Franz Jagerstatter was one of them in the 20th century.

An Austrian who experienced a religious awakening in his twenties, he once said that "I can say from my own experience how painful life often is when one lives as a halfway Christian; it is more like vegetating than living."

Jagerstatter believed Nazism to be evil, and refused to report for military duty. Though family and religious leaders tried to change his mind, Jagerstatter stood fast. He was tried by a military tribunal, convicted of being an enemy of the state and, on August 9, 1943, beheaded.

Sixty-four years later, a crowd of thousands, including his widow and daughters, witnessed his beatification and heard his courageous faith called a challenge and an encouragement to all.

The Lord stood near (Paul) and said, "Keep up your courage! For just as you have testified for Me in Jerusalem, so you must bear witness also in Rome." (Acts 23:11)

Bless me with a discerning conscience and great courage, Mighty Lord of Jacob.

Take Care

As people live longer, more adult children find themselves in the role of personal caregiver for their elderly parents. Or, if they live far away, they struggle to find the best local caregivers available to assist their frail parents or other relatives.

Writing in *Psychotherapy Networker* magazine, Katy Butler describes the problems she faced and the lessons she learned as family roles evolved.

1. Changing family circumstances can be challenging and stressful. Caregivers need to recognize when they need help and how to get it.
2. Support groups can help. Search on line. For example, look under Alzheimer's disease.
3. Work on improving communication. Siblings need to share tasks and to discuss problems.
4. Don't neglect your own spouse and children. Strive for balance.

Balance is always important in all we do.

Honor your father and your mother. (Mark 7:10)

Ancient of Days, guide and support the adult children of aged parents as they care for them.

Summer Camp's Simple Pleasures

"I came up with the name Kindle because my goal was to light a fire of hope in these kids," says Eva Payne, founder of Project Kindle.

Now a thriving non-profit organization offering fun and support to children and families with HIV and AIDS, it started small as Camp Kindle while Payne was still in college. As a student, Payne became involved in the Nebraska AIDS Project. She combined that commitment and her fond memories of summer camp—every summer from third grade through high school, she'd attended camp and loved it—and discovered her mission in life.

"Setting goals, trying things I never would have otherwise, being away from my parents and becoming independent—you can't put a price on any of that," she says.

Now Payne enlists the help of her husband, three children and various professionals and volunteers to keep her project going.

In whom can you kindle hope?

The hope of the righteous ends in gladness. (Proverbs 10:28)

Who needs hope, Lord of all hopefulness? How can I enkindle hope in them?

Tea Time

If you're stressed out and gulp coffee on the run, slow down. Take a tea break. Once you switch to tea you join the legions, present and past, who have long appreciated the personal and social rituals of tea drinking.

According to author and educator Juliet Schor, more and more Americans are "downsizing" in the sense that they have come to value their time more than money. In *The Overspent American, Upscaling, Downshifting,* and the *New Consumer,* she writes that people with this mindset "are growing and mainstreaming."

For the many busy people who feel they must multi-task, slowing down isn't easy. If that describes you, try for a more harmonious life. And since tea is associated with a healthier lifestyle and has health benefits, try it, too.

Who knows, you might just find that both are your cup of tea.

There is nothing better for mortals than to eat and drink, and find enjoyment in their toil. This also, I saw, is from...God, for apart from Him who can eat or who can have enjoyment? (Ecclesiastes 2:24-25)

Remind me, Jesus, Carpenter and Rabbi, that I do not live to work but work to live.

Love Knows No Bounds

Many people are familiar with *Access Hollywood* TV host, Nancy O'Dell. But did you know that her best friend and aunt has Down Syndrome?

And it was because of her Aunt Ellen that O'Dell became an active member of Best Buddies while a reporter in Miami. O'Dell wanted to work with people who were making a difference for those with challenges. Through Best Buddies they can find and maintain friendships and be mainstreamed.

O'Dell's gratitude for her Aunt Ellen's friendship is her motivation for advocacy. She says, "I hope I've helped give a few people that opportunity. It's only a way of returning the friendship and love my Aunt Ellen gave me."

In friendship, no disability should be seen, only the lovable person.

A friend loves at all times. (Proverbs 17:17)

Help us ensure that the differently-abled and the handicapped are included, not excluded, from mainstream life and friendships, eternal and all-embracing God.

Surprisingly Welcoming

Upon the death of philanthropist Brooke Astor at age 105, *New York Times* writer Frances Kiernan wrote that her own grandmother "was cut from the same cloth." Like Astor, Kiernan's grandmother was a woman who found New York City, in spite of its demanding pace, "surprisingly welcoming." It became the place where her "means, imagination and stamina" came alive.

In what environment do *your* means, imagination and stamina come alive? We are called to love people. This can be demanding sometimes. Yet these strong women took advantage of the demand, transforming it into a condition that was "surprisingly welcoming" to cultivating the essence of themselves.

If today looks like a bleak environment in which to show love, trust in the Holy Spirit who fills you.

And when he spoke to me, a spirit entered into me and set me on my feet; and I heard him speaking to me. (Ezekiel 2:2)

Lord, You are my Provider. You have provided me today with a time and place to realize and demonstrate love. I pray that I recognize it and use it to Your glory.

Seven Deadly Virtues?

If someone asked you to name the traditional list of Seven Deadly Sins, you'd probably come up with pride, sloth, gluttony, greed, anger, lust and envy. But writer Ashley Cooper has another take on the subject:

"Truth, if it becomes a weapon against persons.

"Beauty, if it becomes vanity.

"Love, if it becomes possessive.

"Loyalty, if it becomes blind, careless trust.

"Tolerance, if it becomes indifference.

"Self-confidence, if it becomes arrogance.

"Faith, if it becomes self-righteous."

If we allow it, virtues can be perverted. Depend on God's grace to guide you in avoiding the Seven Deadly Sins and in living the virtues.

Live your life in a manner worthy of the Gospel of Christ. (Philippians 1:27)

Beloved God, fill my being with Your grace so that all I do will be done in You and for You.

Addition by Subtraction

Often it's not what we add to our life that makes it better, but what we eliminate.

Cheryl Richardson, a life coach, speaker and author, offers these steps—a plus and minus of activities and goals—to help you improve your life.

- **Make an "add" list.** Identify three goals you'd like to add—a new close friend, a better job, more time with family, as examples.

- **Start subtracting.** Create a second list of three "energy zappers" that you're ready to eliminate.

- **Take action.** Break each item on your "subtract" list into smaller tasks that you can tackle over a month's time. Then get going—and don't procrastinate. Little by little, you'll be welcoming your life's new "additions."

God's gifts are all around us. We just need to make room to add them into our lives—and into our hearts.

> **The necessities of life are water, bread, and clothing, also a house to assure privacy. (Sirach 29:21)**

> *I must decrease, Lord, so that it is Your presence that others see in me.*

The Power of Nature

"Nature is a healing for all of us," says Michael Muir, great-grandson of the famous naturalist John Muir.

He heads Access Adventure, a program which helps disabled people enjoy the outdoors. A horse lover since childhood, Muir co-developed a horse-drawn carriage with a battery-powered electric lift. These light-weight carriages can take "someone who is housebound and put them in the beauty of nature," says Muir, who has multiple sclerosis and uses a cane.

Not only the disabled benefit. An able-bodied 18-year-old whose mother worried that he was depressed and couch-bound became a volunteer after enjoying carriage rides. He now cleans and harnesses the horses weekly.

Michael Muir helps show that God uses "the mountains, and all nature, to bring hope and healing."

You stretch out the heavens...make springs gush...by the streams the birds...have their habitation; they sing among the branches. ...You have made the moon to mark the seasons; the sun knows its time for setting. (Psalm 104:2,10,12,19)

Help me find that deep-down peace and healing which You offer in nature, Savior.

Breaking the Smoking Habit

Despite dire health warnings, people still smoke. In fact, even after someone decides to quit, it's not easy to do. Paul McKenna, a self-help expert, offers this advice:

1. Don't wait. If you can stop smoking for a day or two, you can stop, period.

2. Change your perspective. Create a strong visual image of "the horrible future that awaits" you if you don't quit.

3. Imagine a better life. Your imagination is a more powerful tool than logic.

4. Will yourself into revulsion. Learn to associate smoking with strong negatives as bad taste, hacking cough, yellow teeth, etc.

5. Fight cravings. Rate them on a scale of 1 to 10. Using techniques such as distraction, delay acting on cravings.

Give your body a chance to be healthy. Begin today.

There is no wealth better than health of body. (Sirach 30:16)

Jesus who healed the sick, help those who smoke tobacco to stop.

Creative Arts, Changing Lives

When she was 21, Mary-Mitchell Campbell defied death and realized that she would never be the same.

"It was a turning point. I felt there was definitely something I was supposed to do," she says of surviving a serious car crash unscathed. It took time for her to find her mission.

Ultimately, she put her career as a Broadway musical director and Julliard professor on hold to volunteer at an orphanage in India. These days, Campbell is involved in various charitable endeavors but continues her creative pursuits.

"It's important to show I can do both, still have a fruitful career and be an active and responsible citizen," said the musical director for the Tony-winning revival of *Sweeney Todd*. "My success with my career is a byproduct of my helping other people. God rewards you in ways you weren't expecting."

Bravo!

Guard me as the apple of the eye; hide me in the shadow of Your wings. (Psalm 17:8)

God, thank You for protecting us as a hen shelters her chicks beneath her outstretched wings.

A Blessing Disguised as a Failure

A young high school graduate couldn't believe it when her plans to go out-of-state for college collapsed weeks before classes were to begin.

"I was appalled that all my hard work in high school, all my faith in God and others to take care of my needs, had come to this: nothing. Or so it seemed," she later said.

She stayed in-state and went to a small private university near home. She started out frustrated and dissatisfied, but was transformed by the guidance of loving family and friends and inspiring professors. "The meaning of God's keeping me at home became even more clear when my father passed away unexpectedly," she continued.

God has plans for us that we may not understand, but they are always powered by His love.

Do not be conformed to this world, but be transformed by the renewing of your minds, so you may discern what is the will of God — what is good, acceptable and perfect. (Romans 12:2)

I praise Your name, Jesus, because I know Your plans for me are infinitely better than my own.

What They Say

Do you gossip? We may not like to admit it, but most of us do. We probably don't even think twice about it. Yet, focusing on the negative in other people and spreading stories, whether true or false, hurts their reputations—and our character.

And just because we're repeating what we've heard is no excuse. Writer Ellen Wilcox Wheeler put it this way:

"Have you heard of the terrible family They,

And the dreadful venomous things They say?

Why, half the gossip under the sun,

If you trace it back, you will find begun

In that wretched House of They."

Sadly, They is really us. Next time, speak up on behalf of the person being savaged or say that it's nobody's business and walk away. What you say is always up to you.

A gossip goes about telling secrets, but one who is trustworthy in spirit keeps a confidence. (Proverbs 11:13)

My Redeemer, forgive me for the times I've spoken unjustly or unkindly about others. Help me speak about people with the same respect I'd want for myself.

Living — Really Living

Sara Widener was just 18 when she was diagnosed with brain and spinal cancer. She hasn't spent her time thinking about dying since she learned her diagnoses. Rather, she has been living as never before.

"Cancer changed my perspective on life," says Widener. "I thought I was happy before, but I didn't fully realize how precious and beautiful my life really is."

While she has engaged in some pursuits she always wanted to experience, like rock climbing and skydiving, living life to the fullest also includes a focus on serving others. She and her mother Barbara have raised money to provide cancer treatments for the poor. In addition, Widener has worked to raise awareness and funds for the Pediatric Brain Tumor Consortium.

Transforming devastating news into a renewed zest for life takes courage. Live with courage all your days.

Do not fear, greatly beloved, you are safe. Be strong and courageous! (Daniel 10:19)

Counselor, in my darkest hour embolden me with faith.

Music to My Ears

If you're a music lover, then you'll be happy to know that listening is good for you. "Cutting-edge research reveals how music can help you ease pain, think smarter, feel energized, and fight disease," notes Jordan Lite in *Prevention* Magazine.

- In pain? Combine music and guided imagery. "Music seems to stimulate the release of pain-masking endorphins," according to a music therapy professor.

- Trouble breathing? Try singing or playing a wind instrument to relax while increasing your breathing capacity.

- Can't sleep? Make music part of your daily sleep ritual.

- Feeling depressed? Experts recommend listening to up-tempo music undisturbed for 10 to 20 minutes.

All these potential benefits—and more—from something you already enjoy no doubt leaves you feeling this is "music to your ears."

Praise God...with trumpet...lute and harp...with tambourine and dance...with strings and pipe... with clanging (and)...loud clashing cymbals! (Psalm 150:1,3,4,5)

Thanks for the gift of music, Divine Creator.

Crisis and Opportunity

"I grew up believing that's what you do—work hard and try to make the world a little better," says Dr. Karen DeSalvo. She lives by that philosophy.

Immediately after Hurricane Katrina, Dr. DeSalvo treated traumatized survivors in New Orleans even as she realized that "there will be tens of thousands of people like this who've lost everything."

DeSalvo saw an opportunity to help rebuild the health-care system by developing a network of neighborhood clinics. She and her colleagues established 18 Partnership for Access to Healthcare (PATH) clinics where 18,000 patients are seen each month.

The city's health-care system is still hurting, but Dr. DeSalvo knows that, "everyday, people are getting care who would not otherwise get it. Even on the worst days, something good is happening here." Can you say that about your work?

Paul...went to Corinth. There he found a Jew named Aquila...with his wife Priscilla...and because he was of the same trade, he stayed with them, and they worked together—by trade they were tentmakers. (Acts 18:1,2,3)

Let it be said of my work, Carpenter of Nazareth, that "something good is happening here."

From The Bronx, and Proud of It

People who grow up in New York City love to reminisce about their borough and its neighborhoods.

The borough of The Bronx, for instance, has various ethnic communities where most natives will happily share stories about their childhood playgrounds, their schools, the rough times they and The Bronx endured and the restaurants and shops they continue to frequent.

Bronx native and author Stephen Welles, who wrote *Streets of Honor,* tells about the 1970s, when many youngsters either got into drugs and criminal activity or struggled for a way out. Msgr. John Gallagher of Yonkers' St. Paul the Apostle Church, remembers growing up in the 1930s and 40s with his severely disabled younger brother near Yankee Stadium.

What shaped your childhood? The times? The people? Your city and your neighborhood? Understanding where you came from gives insight into who you are today.

He made His home in a town called Nazareth, so that what had been spoken through the prophets might be fulfilled, "He will be called a Nazorean." (Matthew 2:23)

May I be a positive force in a child's life, Jesus Christ.

Keeping Your Brain in Shape

Have you ever forgotten where you parked? Or had a difficult time remembering if you mailed a letter?

Don't despair! Often small lapses in memory are simple forgetfulness and there's no need to worry about Alzheimer's or other serious problems. However, there are a few steps you can perform to keep your mind in shape.

- Before trying to remember something new, clear your mind of other thoughts.
- Get more sleep! Feeling well-rested keeps you thinking sharper.
- Maintain a Brain-Healthy Diet. Eat foods that are known for anti-inflammatory and antioxidant properties.
- Exercise your whole body.

These four tips can keep your mind feeling sharp and rejuvenated. Take good care of you body, mind and spirit.

The mind is the root of all conduct...good and evil, life and death. (Sirach 37:17, 18)

Holy Spirit, guide our efforts to remain mentally young.

From Life Experience to Helping Others

Have you heard of the movie *American Gangster* or the documentary *Mr. Untouchable?* Now meet the children of the men involved

Francine Lucas-Sinclair, daughter of *American Gangster* Frank Lucas, lost her parents to the criminal justice system at a young age. Along with the support of Nicole and Ebony Barnes, daughters of *Mr. Untouchable* Nicky Barnes, she has founded Yellow Brick Roads. This organization helps to mentor and support children whose parents are or were imprisoned.

All three women believe in helping children thrive despite difficult situations. That support could be in helping with homework or contributing financially. These women work to ensure that innocent children have a future filled with joy and love.

Every child deserves a future full of opportunities. So, do all you can to help real children have a future full of hope.

I know the plans I have for you, says the Lord, plans for your welfare and not for harm, to give you a future with hope. (Jeremiah 29:11)

Lord of all hope, make us Your instruments.

Seniors in Cyberspace?

Some people think "surfing the net" is a pastime reserved only for the young who are considered more techno-savvy than older adults. But a group of seniors in Maryland are offering proof that the online revolution is cross-generational.

The Elder Wisdom Circle, a nationwide organization of seniors offering free advice on family, social and other personal issues, provides its service through the Internet. Advice seekers type their queries on the group's web site, then an elder replies.

The self-dubbed "cyber-grandparents" are web-savvy and eager to help, and field questions ranging from general inquiries on everyday matters to serious topics affecting troubled teens or individuals with marriage, health or financial troubles.

The members of the Elder Wisdom Circle use their accumulated know-how to help others—in a contemporary, efficient and economical way. What could be more "hip" than that?

You shall rise before the aged, and defer to the old; and you shall fear your God: I am the Lord. (Leviticus 19:32)

Reinforce my respect for the elderly, Ancient of Days.

Dog Divers Save Swimmers

If you are fortunate enough to visit the beaches of Italy this summer, you'll notice some unusual rescue workers: Newfoundland and Labrador retrievers.

The dogs work with human partners from the Coast Guard to save swimmers from drowning. They get two years of training and only the top dogs become part of the program. The canine rescuers are capable of diving from boats, the beach and even helicopters. In one recent year the dogs saved 70 people.

Newfoundland and Labrador retrievers are well suited to their task. Strong swimmers whose thick layers of fat provide insulation against the cold, they also react very quickly when they see someone in the water. Newfoundlands' front paws are even webbed!

The human-animal bond is amazing. Mutual loyalty and respect offer rewards to all.

God formed every animal of the field and every bird...and brought them to the man to see what he would call them; and whatever the man called every living creature, that was its name. (Genesis 2:19)

Generous Father, thank You for the gift of all Your creatures, especially our companions.

One Man's Work For Normalcy

The after effects of Hurricane Katrina are still felt by many. Cyril Crutchfield, for one, struggles to give the teens of Port Sulphur, Louisiana, a sense of normalcy.

Because of the hurricane, the high school had to be reconstructed. But Crutchfield, the football coach of South Plaquemines High School, tries to help players despite lack of electricity, food or housing. At the beginning of the season, the team survived on sandwiches and would often have to practice before the sun rose and continue after it set.

Crutchfield continues to ensure that the athletes have as regular a life as possible in the prolonged post-Katrina devastation.

One man's hard work is an example to all. What are we doing to ensure that children and teens have an ordered life come what may?

Give good gifts to your children. (Luke 11:13)

Abba, remind parents that the best gifts they can give their children are love, respect security and stability.

Recognizing the Marvelous

An email anecdote told the story of a very special baseball game.

A neighborhood team said "yes" to a father's request to let his young disabled son play, and the other team purposely allowed the boy to win the game with a grand slam. The players brought a piece of true love and humanity into the world to a youngster who had known more than his share of pain, and a father who wanted his son to know some fun and joy.

Isn't it marvelous how God can knit the ordinary and the extraordinary together into one fabric? Neither operates alone; the ordinary in isolation is drab; the extraordinary in isolation is daunting. Together, they enable us to realize who we are and why we are.

"I have uttered what I did not understand, things too wonderful for me, which I did not know." (Job 42:3)

O God, I want to dwell in Your marvelous light! Open my whole being to Your wonder. Let Your will be done in me.

Going Back to a New Home

With Hurricane Katrina's damage to people's homes along the Gulf Coast, many continue to remain homeless and living in trailers. However, thanks to the efforts of nonprofit foundations and business contributions, residents from those destroyed areas are getting their lives back.

Architecture for Humanity, a group founded by Cameron Sinclair and Kate Stohr, focuses not only on designing practical homes which take flooding into consideration, but they also offer architects who will design these homes. Their Biloxi Model Home Program has given people like Karen Parker help with her family home so she and her six children can move on with their lives.

Parker had considered not going back to where her family lived before the hurricane, but she couldn't bear to leave her home.

Do all you can to reach out to those in need of decent, permanent homes.

Return to your home and declare how much God has done for you. (Luke 8:39)

Redeemer, show us how to return to our true home.

Creative Grandparenting

Grandparents offer extremely important relationships to their grandchildren. Their homes are often the ones youngsters visit on weekends, holidays and vacations; in which grandchildren feel precious, on top of the world. For grandparents trying to bond with their grandchildren, try these few tips:

- Share your delight in nature through walks and conversation.
- Create time for art: provide water colors, modeling clay, crayons or other craft supplies to be creative together.
- Take part in education: trips to the library or museums.
- Take an interest in their interests! You'll learn a lot.
- Allow them to invite friends on outings with you.
- Lastly, lots of love, attention and care go a long way.

Grandparents understand that your grandchildren love you for who you are. Enjoy their youth and, most of all, give loving, liberating support.

Grandchildren are the crown of the aged. (Proverbs 17:6)

Bless children and their grandparents, Abba.

Teachers Also Learn

Joyce Nutta couldn't understand why her classroom of adult students, all of whom were education majors, didn't share her passion for learning. From the first day they were late, disinterested, distracted, even hostile. Half didn't take notes.

She prayed, "Lord, give me patience and wisdom." When that didn't work, she talked to her husband. He suggested, "Pray for them. Pray for each and every student, envisioning them happy and successful."

During the next class, Nutta looked at each student and considered the daily stresses they were under trying to get an education while holding down jobs and raising families. And she prayed for them individually. Slowly, her students began to change. So did she—seeing them as individuals trying to better themselves.

Education is a duet: teachers and students need to work together and respect each other to achieve success.

A disciple is not above the teacher. (Matthew 10:24)

Open students' minds to the value of obtaining an education, Divine Master.

Doctors Who 'Pay It Forward'

After Hurricane Katrina, doctors from around the country volunteered their expertise. Among them were surgeons meeting at the American College of Surgeons Clinical Congress. They took two days to help clear out the former St. Cecilia School so that a neighborhood health clinic could be built. The surgeons called ripping out ceiling tiles and flooring among other chores, "Operation Giving Back."

Dr. David Knight, a general surgeon from Waterbury, Connecticut, said, "You do something for somebody with the idea that they will take it and be an example for somebody else and go on and do good things." Knight hopes that his work will inspire others to help in the efforts to build a better future for the people who suffered from the hurricane.

Your good example can prove inspirational in your own neighborhood.

Let us set an example. (Judith 8:24)

May we be inspired by others' good example. And may we in turn set a good example for others, Spirit of Wisdom.

Two Ways of Seeing

Isn't it amazing what a difference our attitudes make?

For 17 years, Bessie Pender had been a custodian at an elementary school where she cleaned class rooms, offices, bathrooms, and more.

According to a *New York Times* article, for seven years she had also attended college, finally earning her degree in education. Her dream was to teach in the same school where she'd mopped floors. But when Pender applied, the principal refused, saying that because everyone knew her in one role, they wouldn't accept her in another.

Then a former teacher, Peggie Tomlinson, who had become a principal at a different school, hired Pender as a fifth grade teacher. Tomlinson remembered the care with which Pender had always worked and believed that she'd be an excellent teacher—and offer an inspiring example to students.

Two principals, two attitudes. Look for the positive in all circumstances.

Truthful lips endure forever. (Proverbs 12:19)

It's easy to get see the worst in circumstances, Blessed Trinity. Remind me to look for the best in myself and others.

The Scandal of Poverty

A writer recently said, "We don't often drive through the lower part of town where the minorities live...or work in the down-town soup kitchen...the poor are invisible."

But poverty in our communities is visible — if we just open our eyes. Here are some facts:

- One in four jobs pays less than a poverty level income.
- 46 million Americans have no medical insurance.
- 40% of the aged live on less than $18,000 a year—including Social Security.
- 26% of the children of immigrant parents live in poverty; 19% if parents are U.S. born
- 25.9% of Native Americans are poor; 46% are unemployed.
- 40% of families spend more than one-third of their income for rent.
- Median income decreased $2,000 between 2001 and 2005.

The scandal of poverty, is all around you. Educate yourself. Live simply. Volunteer. Vote. Lobby. Do all you can to lessen poverty.

Open your hand to the poor and needy neighbor in your land. (Deuteronomy 15:11)

What can we do to ease poverty, Jesus?

Nice Guys Finish First

Nice guys no longer finish last in today's competitive businesses when they are influenced by positive social interactions rather than harsh assertiveness.

A Gallup poll "found that workers' productivity is directly related to their relationship with their supervisor—in other words, those who viewed their boss favorably accomplished more."

Nice does not mean naïve, nor does it mean weak. Nice simply means showing human kindness; living positively with a clear conscience; and showing compassion for others.

How do you acquire these powers of "nice"? Here are some tips: help your enemies; turn adversaries into allies; be empathetic; and tell the truth.

Owe no one anything, except to love one another. (Romans 13:8)

Lord, help me achieve spiritual, professional, and social success by treating others, each and every one, with heartfelt respect.

Capable of Amazing Accomplishments

Holly McCamant grew up in a family of nine children. Finances were tight. Although she wanted to go to college, she had to defer that dream and get a job.

Money was still tight 25 years later when she was divorced and raising six children alone, but she was determined to fulfill her academic aspirations. Since her children were older she "saw it as now or never."

So, at age 44, McCamant enrolled at the University of Montana with a full course load, a full-time job and full-time parenting responsibilities. "My schedule was nuts," she acknowledges. But eventually she received her degree, found a new position and married a "good, supportive man."

She says, "I feel like I have so much to offer, and I showed my kids that we are all capable of accomplishing amazing things if we put our minds to it."

You can do great things if you persevere.

The Lord was my support. (Psalm 18:18)

Abba, support all working mothers.

For the Good of Others

In the wake of Hurricane Katrina, many kinds of aid were needed. The Common Ground Legal Collective provided support by researching insurance claims for displaced residents, canvassing neighborhoods concerning possible class action suits, and more.

Nineteen students from Marquette University Law School volunteered to travel from Wisconsin to New Orleans as part of the project in the summer of 2007. The law students stayed in the ravaged Upper Ninth Ward.

"Many sections of the city look as if the levees broke a few weeks ago, not two years ago," says group leader Terry Mambu. "The loss and suffering is a devastating crime against humanity."

Many volunteers became convinced of the need for more pro bono work for poor people not only on the Gulf coast, but around the country.

Every person can contribute time and talent to benefit those in sometimes desperate need.

As you did it one of the...members of My family, you did it to Me. (Matthew 25:40)

Jesus, let me never forget that I have a responsibility to all my suffering brothers and sisters. Show me how You want me to serve.

Singing the Blues Again — and Liking It

In the 1970s, Elliott Glick was in his 20s and performing on New York's coffeehouse circuit. As he traveled from club to club with his guitar and original songs, he also took his dreams of making it big in the music world.

Then came marriage and children—and the reality of supporting his family. The songwriting and café singing stopped.

More than two decades later, with his children grown and now grandchildren in the mix, Glick added musicians to the roster of artists showcased at his City Island, New York, gallery. Soon it was like the coffeehouses of his youth.

Inspired by these musicians, Glick started writing songs and then performing, first at his own club and later at other venues. Life had come full circle.

For most of us, life is not a straight line. But if we stick with it, we'll find the way back to our center.

To the sound of musicians at the watering places...repeat the triumphs of the Lord. (Judges 5:11)

Guide my feet, Divine Master, that I might always find my way back to You.

Leading by Following

The heart of leadership is service: putting yourself on the line for what you believe and speaking out for the good of others. The best leaders also know how to follow.

"Jesus is the ultimate example of followership," says Pastor Todd Krygsheld of the Ebenezer Reformed Church in Holland, Michigan. "With His not-My-will-but Your-will-be-done heart, Jesus followed His Father's will… humbling Himself and becoming obedient to death.

"He knew that in order for His disciples to be leaders they first needed to be followers. They followed Jesus, watched Jesus, listened to Jesus, and were taught by Jesus. In the Great Commission, He called them to 'make disciples of all nations'." (Matthew 28:19)

"Leadership," Pastor Krygsheld adds, "is not something we go into but rather grow into as we follow Christ more fully."

Be a leader—Jesus' way.

Let the same mind be in you that was in Christ Jesus, who, though He was…God, did not regard equality with God as something to be exploited. …He humbled Himself and became obedient… even (to) death on a cross. (Philippians 2:5-6,8)

Jesus, guide us in being servants and leaders.

Ole!

Entertaining, colorful, passionate—flamenco dancing is also historic. The word flamenco itself is the Spanish word for "Flemish." It's said that when Spanish Emperor Charles V returned home from Flanders in 1517, he began using the term to describe those in his court lacking in social graces.

Others insist that the word comes from the Arabic for fugitive peasants, a sign of the Moors' impact on Spanish life. Still others maintain that flamenco pays homage to the flamingo, whose erect stature is mimicked by the dancers themselves.

Flamenco permeates Spanish popular culture. In the late 20th century, a spate of schools opened to teach and preserve the art of flamenco.

Art and music are windows into a people's culture and history. Enjoy and support the arts. Celebrate your own creativity.

I have filled him with divine spirit, with ability, intelligence, and knowledge...to devise artistic designs, to work in gold, silver, and bronze, in cutting stones for setting, and in carving wood, in every kind of craft. (Exodus 31:3,4-5)

Inspire the artist in each of us, Creator of all, who paints sunrises and sunsets; birds' plumage; flowers and fruits.

Life, Love and Choices

It's unfortunate that we don't always realize how important certain people are to us until we lose them.

Frances Cangialosi felt that way about her sister Maggi. In *Bits & Pieces* she wrote that their mother had died when Maggi was nine and she herself was still a baby. Since the older girl helped raise the younger, the sisters' relationship was close, though somewhat turbulent,

It wasn't until they were adults and Maggi developed breast cancer that the younger sister understood all her older sister had been to her: mother, sister, best friend, confidante, sage, and spiritual advisor.

In a letter written shortly before she died, Maggi wrote: "Nothing is as precious as life, to be alive to make choices. Life is the result of the choices we make."

Now, Frances Cangialosi tries to make every choice the best choice. Each of us would benefit if we did the same.

Wine and music gladden the heart, but the love of friends is better than either. (Sirach 40:20)

Compassionate Father, open our eyes to Your great gift, the people with whom You surround us. Help us appreciate them.

Petite Protesters Parade Their Pleas

It seems it's not only adults who can become politically active these days.

Baby Bloc, a Vancouver-based non-profit organization, not only encourages parents to take their kids along when they're making a political statement, but wants to facilitate the practice.

Baby Bloc wants to promote a greater understanding between law enforcement officials and protesters so that civilly conducted protests can remain safe for children. They plan to create secure areas where youngsters can have snacks and entertainment while their parents engage in peaceful, lawful activism. The idea is to encourage parents of young children to be politically involved.

Civic activism can take many forms, the most critical of which is voting. Be sure to exercise your right to vote.

I have set before you today life and prosperity, death and adversity. ...Choose life. (Deuteronomy 30:15, 19)

Remind us, gracious God, that, as it says in the U.S. Declaration of Independence, governments derive their "just power from the consent of the governed."

Reaching for the Sky

"Look, God, I'm trying my best. I don't know what else to do. It seems so pointless. Was I just being naïve to think I could make a difference?" These were the painful thoughts of one young woman after a particularly hard week.

Jenn Gentlesk recalls life after graduation from Princeton. As a volunteer with the Franciscan Volunteer Ministry, she was assigned to teach at a women's prison and a local elementary school, direct English as a second language courses and visit a nearby nursing home.

While she was still frustrated and feeling as though she had not made any difference, Gentlesk broke her foot. The month away from work gave her time to come to terms with herself and her desire to serve. By the time her foot healed, she was renewed with the vigor to make a difference.

During times of doubt, have faith in God to help you.

If you have faith and do not doubt...even if you say to this mountain, 'Be lifted up and thrown into the sea,' it will be done. Whatever you ask for in prayer with faith, you will receive." (Matthew 21:21-22)

God, I am trying grow in faith. Help me!

When You Need Help

If you've ever had trouble asking for help, be assured you're not alone.

For many people, asking colleagues or friends for help is difficult because they don't want to appear dependent, weak or incompetent. Also, they're afraid the other person will take too much control.

"There is a tendency to act as if it's a deficiency," said Garret Keizer, author of *Help: The Original Human Dilemma*. "There is an understandable fear that if you let your guard down, you'll get hurt."

Quoting Keizer and others in a *New York Times* column, Alina Turgend says that many of us either don't know the best ways to ask for help or we go to the wrong person.

People want to help. Don't be afraid to ask for it. But find the right way, and the right time. And be sure to reciprocate.

Kindred and helpers are for a time of trouble. (Sirach 40:24)

Remind us, Holy Spirit, to be gracious and modest when helping others.

Redemption for Two

Finding redemption after a life of bad choices can be extraordinarily hard. Meet two people who not only learned from their mistakes, but also found love.

Donnie Andrews, once a stickup man, had been imprisoned for murder. Fran Boyd was a heroin addict focused on her next fix. Andrews and Boyd met through a police officer who believed that Andrews could help Boyd. The couple fell in love and married.

Andrews is now working on the anti-gang outreach program of Baltimore's Bethel A.M.E. Church. Boyd visits her old haunts and tries to convince others to give up drugs. She also helps the local hospital's HIV prevention program.

By God's grace, Boyd and Andrews were able to find redemption and love as a couple and to help others in need. Is it time you put your troubles behind you, embraced God's blessings— and helped others do the same?

If the many died through the one man's trespass, much more surely have the grace of God and the free gift in grace of the one man, Jesus Christ, abounded for the many. (Romans 5:15)

Thank You, Jesus, for Your gift of Eternal Life. Help us to accept and live Your gift.

Canines in the Cubicles

A recent memo at a Memphis marketing agency signaled a new trend hitting the American workplace—dogs at the office.

The staff of a Santa Monica ad agency consists of 55 humans—and eight dogs! The pets were originally brought in as a form of inspiration for the agency's then-top priority project, a pet-supply company's advertising campaign. When that project ended, it was decided that the dogs should stay.

Why? Simple. Says a company president, "They lighten the mood of the office," and relieve stress.

While the patter of paws could occasionally be heard in American offices on "casual Fridays" or the day before a holiday weekend, the trend is now broadening to regular workdays.

There are many natural, effective ways to help mitigate stress and its effects. How do you manage stress in your life? Be sure it's as healthy as petting your favorite dog or cat.

In...rest you shall be saved; in quietness and in trust shall be your strength. (Isaiah 30:16)

Strengthen those overwhelmed by stress, Father.

From Giving...Happiness and Health

According to bioethicist Stephen Post writing in *Body + Soul,* "Give a little every single day, and you'll live a happier, healthier, and longer life." Some examples:

- Go beyond limiting self-labels. You are more than your current role in life.

- Be genuinely happy at another's good fortune.

- Give what you need. Need friends? Be a friend. Struggling to overcome an addiction? Help fellow strugglers.

- Use the news to guide you to where help is needed most. Food pantries and soup kitchens struggling with less food and fewer volunteers? Organize a food drive at your church. Volunteer.

- Find your niche. Don't just help others, but connect with your community.

- Empower others with a sense of their infinite value through your generosity. Encourage others to be their best.

Remember: your generosity will return to you in unexpected ways.

The measure you give will be the measure you get, and still more will be given you. (Mark 4:24)

Guide our generosity, Holy Spirit.

A Million Good Ideas

Have you ever seen a million of anything?

Helen Lord taught fourth grade students at St. Catherine's School in Richmond, Virginia. When they said they couldn't visualize what a million meant, Lord suggested that they collect a million dried beans.

It took seven years of work from successive fourth graders to finally reach a million beans. They then took the 120 two-liter soda bottles that contained the beans to a local family shelter to be turned into soup.

Any idea can be made even better. In addition to helping students learn, homeless people benefited from the project. Think about creative ways to improve things for yourself and those around you.

Wisdom is as good as an inheritance. (Ecclesiastes 7:11)

Fill me with the knowledge and wisdom to serve You, Merciful Savior, by serving Your people, especially those most in need.

Ways to Praise

The poet-minister John Donne penned, "No man is an island." Put another way, human beings do not thrive when isolated from each other. And one of the ways we humans help each other grow is through praise. When was the last time you gave another person genuine, heartfelt praise? Gave God genuine, heartfelt praise? Here's writer Chris Widener's questions for reflection on the subject:

- Do you tell your spouse, children and family that you love them each and every day?
- Are you patient with loved ones?
- Have you offered a loved one a positive reflection on him or her in the last 24 hours?
- What character trait in your spouse, child, friend, or co-worker inspires you? Have you communicated your admiration to that person?

Bring joy and fulfillment to your life as well as your loved ones. Aim to praise them sincerely and often.

Great is the Lord, and greatly to be praised; His greatness is unsearchable. (Psalm 145:3)

Remind me to make my life a paean of praise, Precious Lord.

Without Fathers — It's a Crime

It's not just about image, control or power: teens join gangs because they want to be part of a family. In fact, one of the strongest predictors of murders and robbery rates in urban America is the percentage of families headed by single mothers.

Programs that encourage fathers and teens can help. In Boston, the Ella J. Baker House helps youth at high risk for turning to crime to improve reading skills, gain access to jobs and avoid violence.

Married life, family and religion also go a long way to solving the problem, according to researchers Robert Sampson and John Laub.

It's not only important to have positive male and female role models in children's lives, but also to show them that family is about love, support and connectedness.

It was I who taught Ephraim to walk, I took them up in My arms. ...I led them with cords of human kindness, with bands of love. I was to them like those who lift infants to their cheeks. I bent down to them and fed them. (Hosea 11:3,4)

Heavenly Father, bring parents and children together under Your loving Spirit.

The Feminine Side of a Cuppa Joe?

Coffee seems to have acquired a masculine persona. After all, you would be hard-pressed to recall a movie in which a cowboy or a soldier ordered a cup of tea rather than a cup of *java*.

Today, coffee growers in the northern Peruvian Andes are shattering that stereotype. A group of women have come up with a bold solution to ensuring that "fair trade" in the coffee industry translates into "fair profits."

Since 2004, a group of women have been selling their harvests through a women-only collective called Café Femenino. More than 750 women from 50 communities are involved in the project, in which they control the cash and management of the fields themselves and determine how profits are used. Their earnings from sales of coffee-beans have been used to send children to school and improve living conditions.

Every individual is worthy of being treated as a unique individual.

A woman who fears the Lord is to be praised. Give her a share in the fruit of her hands, and let her works praise her in the city gates. (Proverbs 31:30-31)

Instill in me respect for what distinguishes us from one another, Eternal God.

Can't Find it in Stores? Make it Yourself

Like many expectant moms, Beverly Sutherland delighted in the prospect of decorating her baby's room. But for Sutherland, the project took on a special meaning—she wanted her son's room to reflect the family's African-American heritage. "It was important to us to have positive images in our home" to reflect their history and culture, according to Sutherland.

Sutherland's mission became difficult to accomplish, however. Going from store to store, she came up empty handed, as no retailer seemed to carry anything that featured prominent black Americans.

So Sutherland took the matter into her own hands. She created her own line of bedding, curtains and wall art that were both stylish, attractive and culturally significant.

Life doesn't always go our way. More often than not, accomplishing our goals is an uphill climb. But taking a proactive approach to life's challenges, increases chances for success.

Someone asked (Jesus), "Lord, will only a few be saved?" He said to them, "Strive to enter through the narrow door." (Luke 13:23-24)

Embolden me to forge innovative solutions, Jesus, my brother.

Competing For the Best

The Universities of Illinois and Arizona are respectful rivals with the same goal. "We're both trying to change the perception of wheelchair sports," Miriam Ladner, a paralympian and Illinois University graduate told *The New York Times.*

The two universities give scholarships or tuition waivers and have the premier track and road-racing teams for wheelchair athletes in the United States.

It wasn't always so. Dave Herr-Cardillo of Arizona's adaptive athletics programs recalls days when the program was "a bunch of guys in wheelchairs hitting a beach ball to each other in a basement. That was unacceptable. So we changed that."

It takes time, money and effort as well as changes in attitude to include everyone of every ability in athletics. But inclusiveness is what it takes to be the best whether in university athletics or in life.

You shall not revile the deaf or put a stumbling block before the blind; you shall fear Your God: I am the Lord. (Leviticus 19:14)

Remind us that everyone of every ability is worthy of respect, compassionate God.

Delivery of Hope

Most of us take our mail delivery for granted, but homeless people don't. Without a permanent address, they can't get regular deliveries. The U.S. Postal Service offers help.

While general delivery is rarely used in some areas, it remains a vital link in others. In New York City, for example, it's so popular that the main post office maintains a special facility. The system is simple. Senders put the person's name, General Delivery, city, state and zip code on the envelope. Recipients present identification at their local post office to pick up their mail.

For homeless people who need Social Security checks or disability payments, or who want to keep contact with friends or family, the service is a lifeline.

It's easy to forget the many blessings we enjoy. Remember to treat each person you meet with the same dignity you would want to receive.

Whose offspring are worthy of honor? Human offspring...who fear the Lord. (Sirach 10:19)

Remind me to reach out with mercy, empathy and respect to people in need, Father of all.

Spreading Computer Literacy

While more people are getting home computers, 30 million U.S. households don't have one. That means that 39% of Hispanic, 45% of Black, 15% of White and 11% of Asian children may be left behind in a technologically literate world.

Here are just a few solutions to this problem:

- Andrew Rasiej started a program that introduces public school students to computer technology, from navigating the Internet to maintaining aging school computers.

- Half of Brian Crosby's students speak English as a second language; 90% are poor. Crosby uses discarded Apple computers for all his Sparks, Nevada, students' lessons.

- Through a partnership of Cisco and the nonprofit, One Economy, low-cost PCs, monitors and broadband service are made available to low-income students

Help children you know to achieve computer literacy. It will mean a world of difference to their minds and their futures.

Apply your mind to instruction and...knowledge. (Proverbs 23:12)

Bless students and teachers, Holy Spirit.

Wake Up Your Enthusiasm

Do you sometimes find that your day seems humdrum, even boring? You're not the only one to feel apathetic about life. Rabbi Zelig Pliskin offers some words of encouragement:

"Every morning when you wake up, you are given another day of life. This gift of life is precious. To say that it's precious is really a colossal understatement. Being alive is more valuable than anything else that one can own and possess. The greater your appreciation for being alive, the more enthusiastic you will be when wake you up each morning.

"Your Creator gives you life this moment for a reason. Your life is purposeful. Just imagine the enthusiasm you are going to experience when you realize that the Creator and sustainer of the universe is saying to you, 'I am giving you life this very moment. Appreciate it'."

Each moment of life is a gift. Use it well.

What gain have the workers from their toil?...There is nothing better for them than to be happy and enjoy themselves...(to) eat and drink and take pleasure in all their toil. (Ecclesiastes 3:9,12,13)

Creator of all things, thank You for Your generosity to us, Your children. Help us appreciate each and every moment You give us.

Day Care and Much More

"We were young and stupid," recalls Sister Berta Ailer, who, more than 35 years ago, responded with Sister Corita Bussanmas to a working mother's need for daycare.

"How hard can that be?" they thought as they opened their living room and started caring for several neighborhood toddlers and preschoolers.

Today "Operation Breakthrough" serves 650 youngsters and their families in Kansas City, Missouri. Child care is provided along with tutoring, medical care and summer programs. Parents can access housing assistance, GED classes and much more.

The local community respects and supports what has become a multi-million dollar operation. The Kansas City Chiefs pro-football team, for example, regularly helps raise funds. Former daycare kids return as adults to help out.

These nuns responded to a need with enthusiasm. You too can begin to address a problem in your family or neighborhood. Take action.

Blessed are the merciful, for they will receive mercy. (Matthew 5:7)

Inspire our attempts to address needs and resolve problems, Holy Wisdom.

The Value of Friendship

When boys in her freshman high school English class mocked timid African-American Queen Bond, Dominican-American Cristal Pimentel—all 4-feet-11-inches of her—defended her. The friendship of these students: poor, at risk of dropping out, and with minimal skills had begun.

Together they determined to take every opportunity offered: R.O.T.C.; Saturday classes; extra tutoring; writing research papers; reading literature; choir; theater group; free tickets to Broadway shows. The school's assistant principal for humanities mentored them, helped them study for the SAT and apply to colleges through New York State's Educational Opportunity Program.

Bond and Pimentel are the first in their families to earn high school diplomas—with B-plus averages. Bonds says of Pimentel: "I'm so used to her being my support system." Pimental considers Bond and their teachers "the closest I've gotten to a family."

Friendship + native intelligence + hard work = success.

Happy is the one who finds a friend. (Sirach 25:9)

Bless poor, struggling students with faithful friends and caring educators, Jesus, Teacher.

"There is hope"

"Free your mind, free your spirit, free your soul," Peter Brenner said into the microphone. "Let the music take control."

14 years ago, Brenner, then owner of a health food store, was shot seven times during a robbery. Two bullets in his lower spine paralyzed him below the waist, causing periods of excruciating pain. He now lives in the nursing home at New York's Coler-Goldwater Hospital.

In his mid-40s, the Jamaican-American is a DJ whose afternoon reggae music program on WCGH 88.1 FM, "The Beat of the Heart," is broadcast from the hospital.

Brenner says, "For you and you and God knows who. Brooklyn, Queens, Manhattan, Staten Island, all the tri-state area: Big up!" He adds, "Music generates love, clears my mind and lifts my spirit. I could be angry about (my) condition, but I occupy my time doing something positive."

Whatever the negatives in your life, do something positive.

There is hope for a tree, if it is cut down, that it will sprout again, and that its shoots will not cease. (Job 14:7)

Bless us with resiliency and optimism, Holy Spirit.

To Speak or Not to Speak

Sometimes it's hard to judge whether or not speaking up or keeping quiet is the right thing to do. Either way, there is always a chance of hurting someone and making matters worse. Here are some tips from Judith Sills, Ph.D, found in *Family Circle* magazine, to consider when facing this dilemma:

- Give your opinion on a subject, but don't tell other people what to do.
- Refrain from making on-the-spot decisions. Instead, think about the situation carefully before acting.
- Avoid being negative; rather compliment others, focusing on the good.
- Speak up if necessary, but be kind and don't get overly involved.

Whenever there is a situation where you want to be helpful, remember that what you see as useful could have negative consequences. Make sure your words will help, not hurt.

Seek good and not evil. (Amos 5:14)

Help us be helpful, but neither intrusive or disrespectful, compassionate God.

One Step at a Time

You may think you're constantly running around, but do you know how many steps you really take in a day?

While Americans walk an average of 5,300 steps a day, most fitness experts recommend 10,000 steps. According to the *Journal of the American Medical Association*, the simplest way to increase walking is to wear a pedometer.

"These little devices are a great motivational tool," says Dr. Dena Bravata, an internist and senior research scientist at California's Stanford University.

People who regularly wear pedometers walk about 2,000 more steps a day than those who don't. Research shows that pedometer users who set daily goals not only walked more, but also made other improvements such as cutting calories and increasing other physical activities. They also lost weight and reduced their blood pressure.

Each of us has a responsibility to care for our health. Think about little changes that can add up to big benefits.

Health and fitness are better than any gold. (Sirach 30:15)

Jesus, help me look after my physical, mental and spiritual welfare.

The Cross and a Prayer

St. Francis of Assisi was known for his great love of Jesus and his attempt to imitate Him as completely as possible.

"Francis, of course, had a heart very much attuned to the mystery of God's overflowing love," wrote Rev. Jack Wintz, O.F.M., in *St. Anthony Messenger.* "Once, Francis had a vision of Christ looking at him from the cross with such intense and burning love that 'his soul melted', according to his biographer, St. Bonaventure. One can only believe that, after this...every time Francis prayed before a crucifix, he experienced a similar outpouring of God's incredible love."

Francis often said this prayer before a crucifix:

Most High, glorious God, enlighten the darkness of my heart; Give me the right faith, sure hope, and perfect charity. Fill me with understanding and knowledge, that I may fulfill Your command.

Say and contemplate these words.

Like a lamb that is led to the slaughter, and like a sheep that before its shearers is silent, so He did not open his mouth. (Isaiah 53:7)

Jesus, my Redeemer, hold me in Your loving embrace.

Extraordinarily Gifted

Noah Van Niel is no ordinary college football player. Nor is he an ordinary aspiring opera tenor. The Harvard undergraduate is both.

"It's fun to meld the two worlds that society tells us are so different," Van Neil told a *New York Times* reporter.

His unusual mingling of talents emerged from seeing possibilities in small opportunities. Whenever a chance popped up for Van Niel to pursue singing and acting, he recognized it with the attitude, "Wow, I might have a shot at really doing this." And the role given him on the playing field, as a blocker, is one that teammates say he embraces.

Maybe we don't see more people like Van Niel because many don't take advantage of every opportunity. And yet look at how much can be accomplished when confidence and enthusiasm are given a chance.

Since you are eager for spiritual gifts, strive to excel in them for the building up of the church. (1 Corinthians 14:12)

Holy God, help me approach opportunities to excel in and to share my gifts with confidence and eagerness.

Growing Healthy Goals

The goals we set are a lot like children: they need nurturing; they can bring us great joy and fulfillment; they change and evolve over time.

Yet, it's surprising how often we allow our goals to become carved in stone by ignoring their waning value as we ourselves change. Goals manifest both our dreams and values, so what is of paramount importance to us in our 20s may mean less in our middle years. While setting goals is critical, flexibility is also key. Here are some tips to ensure your goals keep up with you.

- **Be specific.** For example, rather than aim to "save money," name a realistic, specific amount.
- **Name your tactics.** How will you actually reach your goal? Do you have the means to achieve what you want?
- **Embrace change.** Remember: goals are signposts of your development, growth and maturation. Do your goals fit you?

The race is not to the swift, nor the battle to the strong, nor bread to the wise, nor riches to the intelligent, nor favor to the skillful; but time and chance happen to them all.
(Ecclesiastes 9:11)

Teach me to accept change with grace and dignity, Lord.

A Clean Sweep for Creation

When the first Earth Day Clean Sweep was held in Michigan's rural Upper Peninsula in 2005, organizers hoped to collect at least one ton of common household poisons, such as pesticides, antifreeze and drain cleaners. They got 46 tons. The next year, an estimated 10,000 people dropped off 320 tons of environmental waste in 27 church parking lots.

Behind Clean Sweep is a partnership of 130 religious congregations—Catholic, Protestant, Jewish and Buddhist—called Earth Keepers, which also works with Native American tribes and other environmental groups.

"We have a responsibility to care for our surroundings," says Bishop Jim Kelsey of the Episcopal Diocese of Northern Michigan, a partner of Earth Keepers, "not only for our own self-preservation, but especially because we are co-inhabitants with the rest of the living beings who are also God's creation."

To be good stewards of our planet, we need first to be good neighbors to all our neighbors.

It is required of stewards that they be found trustworthy. (1 Corinthians 4:2)

Master of all creation, guide me in preserving and protecting all that surrounds me.

Cultural Vandalism

A remote, empty farmhouse offered too much potential for troublemakers to resist. More than 30 teens and adults traveled up a snowy lane past a large blue sign explaining the farmhouse's historic significance.

They brought drugs, beer and rum. Hours later: broken windows, screens, dishes, antiques. An antique chair used for firewood. Spit, vomit, urine, beer, and discharged fire extinguisher residue all over.

According to a Ripton, Vermont, police Sergeant, "one youth asked whether he could use his (police) mug shot on his Facebook page!" Others were indifferent about their vandalism.

To quote the late resident of the house that had been preserved in his honor, poet Robert Frost, "They should have known. They should have known." True. But like too many they were culturally rootless and personally irresponsible.

Cultivate your cultural roots and introduce young people to poetry, novels, non-fiction, plays, concerts and museums. The world will be more human and humane.

Train children in the right way and when old, they will not stray. (Proverbs 22:6)

Help us know and savor the richness of our own culture and others', Lord of nations.

Autumnal Pleasures

A late September or early October day: bright sun; blue skies; mild breezes. It's perfect autumnal—almost summery—weather and a great time for a visit to your local farmers' market.

First, you'll either be spending your dollars in your own community or sending them to one nearby. Second, the cultivation of what you buy will have provided jobs for local farmers and farm workers.

Then there's the environment...

- Yours—if possible, walk or bike to reduce pollution, drive only if you must; bring your own washable canvas sacks to reduce plastic in landfills.

- And the farmers'—the food you buy will have been grown nearby—no need to use lots of fuel transporting it long distances or to over-package the produce.

If you want to leave a better world for your children and grandchildren, make an effort to buy and eat locally.

Do not hate hard labor or farm work, which was created by the Most High. (Sirach 7:15)

Lord of the harvest, prosper and protect farmers and farm workers.

Coming Together

Can old and young mingle together in harmony? Yes!

St. Ann Center for Intergenerational Care in Milwaukee was established by Sister Edna Lonergan, a Franciscan nun. She has devised a program where every week each child has a scheduled activity with an older adult. Another example is the "rock-a-bye club," where adults hold babies three times a week. Sister Edna Lonergan has found that the relationships between the older men and women and the youngsters grow into friendship.

Lonergan says, "When they [elderly] go to nursing homes, everything familiar is gone, and they are isolated from their friends and family. Plus the rest of the family loses out on the wisdom and spirituality of the elderly. They have much to give to the young."

Enjoy the wisdom and friendship of elders.

The glory of youths is their strength, but the beauty of the aged is their gray hair. (Proverbs 20:29)

Bless us with intergenerational respect and harmony, Ancient of Days.

Not "Man's Best Friend" For Nothing

Any dog owner will tell you that dogs offer humans companionship and unconditional love, and are often considered family members. Also, guide and service dogs assist people who are blind or have other challenges.

Canine Assistants, a Georgia-based organization, trains seizure dogs to respond properly and promptly to an owner's epileptic seizure: urging the person to the ground, lying across their chest to prevent standing while still disoriented; retrieving medications; and pressing a button on the phone to call 911, an alert service or a neighbor. The dogs are trained to respond to nearly 90 commands. Thanks to their seizure-response dogs people with epilepsy can often return to their normal daily activities.

Treat animals with respect and care, not just because of all they can do for humankind; animals are as much God's creation as are human beings.

Your steadfast love, O Lord, extends to the heavens, Your faithfulness to the clouds. ...You save humans and animals alike. (Psalm 36:5,6)

Lord, remind us to protect and respect animals.

Emma Lazarus Joins Elite Poets' Corner

If poet Emma Lazarus was alive today, many would assume she was a "one-hit wonder." After all, Lazarus' most famous work remains "New Colossus," which says, "Give me your tired, your poor, your huddled masses yearning to breathe free…I lift my lamp beside the golden door." It's affixed to the pedestal of the Statue of Liberty in New York Harbor.

Lazarus, however, was actually prolific. She wrote several books of poetry, which were met with critical acclaim. According to one London newspaper in 1871, "Miss Lazarus must be hailed by impartial literary criticism as a poet of rare and original power."

Lazarus also wrote a highly praised novel, *Alide: An Episode in Goethe's Life,* which is an adaptation of the German writer's autobiography.

There is so much more to each and every one of us than what's on the surface. Appearances can be deceiving and misleading, and never tell the whole story.

Do not judge by appearances, but judge with right judgment. (John 7:24)

Jesus, remind us that each and every person is unique, complex and deserving of respect.

What's the Point?

Have you ever seriously considered your life's quest?

Writer Charles Swindoll believes that each person needs to have some great mission to give life purpose and focus. In *The Quest for Character*, he writes:

"What is YOUR quest? Do you have a lifelong dream? Anything dominating your life enough to hold your attention?...Some adventurous journey you'd love to participate in...some discovery you long to make...some enterprise you secretly imagine? Without a quest, life is quickly reduced to bleak black and wimpy white, a diet too bland to get anybody out of bed in the morning. A quest fuels our fire. It refuses to let us drift downstream gathering debris. It keeps our mind in gear, makes us press on. All of us are surrounded by, and benefit from, the results of someone else's quest."

Ask yourself how you can achieve your quest.

Whoever does not carry the cross and follow Me cannot be My disciple. (Luke 14:27)

Gracious Savior, guide my path in fulfilling my quest and Your will.

Making Your World Better

Today, Verone Kennedy is a New York City middle school principal and a role model. Yet, no one could have predicted his success.

Kennedy's father ran a dry-cleaners; his mother directed a social services center. But his Brooklyn neighborhood had racial tensions and he described his schools as "unbelievable." He was uninterested in school and failing. A teacher even thought he'd "end up dead or in jail."

Then an art teacher told him he had an aptitude for sketching and painting. He worked on his portfolio and gained confidence that he was good in something. That carried over to academics. With support from this teacher and his mother, Kennedy decided on college.

Later he returned to Crown Heights because "We each have a responsibility and an obligation to better the lives of as many people as we can. There is greatness in those kids."

There's greatness in every child. What can you do about it?

Listen, my children, to instruction. (Sirach 23:7)

Jesus, our teacher, support teachers in their difficult profession.

From Tragedy Comes Innovation

Few know good product design as well as internationally renowned architect and designer Michael Graves. However, even he realized he had more to learn about the subject when, as a result of sickness, he experienced personal mobility limitations.

Graves had been fighting a sinus infection on a business trip when the illness suddenly entered his spinal cord and rendered him paralyzed from the waist down. Literally overnight, Graves found himself at the mercy of what he considered poorly designed medical products.

He set out on a new mission: to design and market well-designed and efficient assistive devices for the disabled, elderly and infirm. Today, Graves' enthusiasm permeates the line of products he has since launched through a medical-device firm to help others in his situation.

So much of life is seeing the glass half-full as opposed to half-empty. Do you have the strength to see opportunity in hardship?

Hope for good things for lasting joy and mercy. (Sirach 2:9)

Through the Lord, our God, all things are possible. Help us, Lord.

Getting Out of Debt

Look at these scary figures:

- In 2003, American consumers owed $1.9773 *trillion*.

- In 2004, the average American household owed about $5,100 in credit card debt.

- Americans spend an average of $1.22 for every $1 they earn.

If your family is part of this unsettling picture, there is hope.

- Keep track of everything you spend for a month. Compare it to your income.

- Look for places where you can make cuts.

- Make a budget or spending plan, whichever sounds better to you.

- Keep a "cash only" policy; avoid credit cards.

- Look for ways you can save money and get better deals on purchases.

Develop a determined, positive mindset which thinks about changes not as sacrifices, but as delayed gratification to achieve your goals.

Better to be poor and walk in integrity than to be crooked in one's ways even though rich. (Proverbs 28:6)

Guide my efforts to care for my family and myself responsibly, Creator of all things.

A Helping Hand

The necessities of life that many people take for granted are overlooked in working-poor families. After school children are alone or in charge of even younger siblings while their parents work long hours at minimum wage jobs. They may not have enough food to eat or only fast food. And if homework isn't done, their education and future success suffers.

But at Paul's Place at St. Paul's Episcopal Church, Delray Beach, Florida, there's help from 4 to 7 pm for 20 Haitian-American children. There's a snack before teachers and volunteers tutor some children in basic math and English. Other youngsters begin their homework.

After dinner at 5:30, there's participatory visual and performing arts, sports or guest speakers talking about their hobbies, lives and transition from Haiti.

The program's full-time director Allen Whittemore says, "Christianity begins at home in your neighborhood." Does yours?

What good is it, my brothers and sisters, if you say you have faith but do not have works? Can faith save you?...Faith by itself, if it has no works, is dead. (James 2:14,17)

Inform my actions with my faith; my faith with my actions, Holy Spirit.

Good News for All

What is the role of missionaries in the 21st century?

They have the dual goal of proclaiming the good news and feeding the poor, according to Cardinal Theodore McCarrick. "The missionary must proclaim Jesus Christ as the only Savior...in the words and the context of the culture to which he or she is sent. The missionary must also seek to transform the social structures of any society where structures of sin and injustice make it difficult for the poor or for women or for any class of people to be given their full respect as human persons."

Maryknoll Father Joseph Veneroso adds this point: "Through word and deed we reflect back to people the presence of God we find in them. By approaching people with reverence, we invite them to join us in repentance and reverence."

Every person, in living out his or her faith, can show others God's immeasurable love.

I will tell of all Your wonderful deeds. I will be glad and exult in You; I will sing praise to Your name, O Most High. (Psalm 9:1-2)

Holy God, let my thoughts, words and deeds proclaim the embrace of Your love for all people.

Crazy Ideas

When girls won the top prizes in a national math and science competition for the first time, it surprised many. But, as biologist Nancy Hopkins of the Massachusetts Institute of Technology said, "Why do people think girls can't do science? Where did this crazy idea come from?"

What about other "crazy ideas" we, as individuals and as a society, keep filed away—ideas we don't say we believe, but ideas we do not deny by our actions. It's important to examine them, because they can prevent us from recognizing the gifts and capacities of other people—and even ourselves.

It's often easier to identify ideas as "crazy"—or unfounded, prejudiced, unloving, self-serving, fearful—when we hear others say them to us. But we need to confront our own thoughts and beliefs and aim to make God's truth our own.

Trust in the Lord with all your heart, and do not rely on your own insight. (Proverbs 3:5)

Lord Jesus, I am hungry for Your truth! Nothing else will do.

A Touch of Class

We've all met people we easily identify as "classy," but still may not be able to define exactly what we mean. Here's how author Howard Ferguson put it in his book, *The Edge*.

"Class never runs scared. It is sure-footed and confident in the knowledge that you can meet life head-on and handle whatever comes along.

"Class never makes excuses. It takes its lumps and learns from past mistakes.

"Class is considerate of others. It knows that good manners are nothing more than a series of small sacrifices. ...

"Class never tries to build up itself by tearing others down.

"Class is already up and need not strive to look better by making others look worse.

"If you have class, you don't need much of anything else. If you don't have it, no matter what else you have—it doesn't make much difference."

In other words, having class means having character.

Endurance produces character, and character produces hope, and hope does not disappoint us. (Romans 5:4-5)

Divine Lord, help me meet my responsibilities head on. Help me count on You so others can count on me.

The Not-So-Secret Fountain of Youth

Diet and exercise truly are the most reliable avenues to longevity and health.

Former caterer Alva Torres, already in her late seventies, wanted to learn ways to avoid future health crises. While participating in a dietary modification trial, she was flabbergasted by her daily fat consumption: "If I'd kept going I'd be a candidate for heart problems," she admits.

Torres began attending a weekly nutrition class and learned to lighten up her cooking and eating. Her new regime helped Torres maintain a healthy weight and lower her cholesterol. Then she wrote a cookbook with traditional recipes on one page, and a healthier version on the facing page so that her daughters and granddaughters could be healthier.

Living healthier doesn't have to mean giving up everything, but it does mean moderation.

Health and fitness are better than any gold. (Sirach 30:15)

Help me enjoy life's bounty in moderation and with good sense, Gracious Father.

Decades of Service

According to the rector of New York's Holy Apostles Episcopal Church and executive director of the Holy Apostles Soup Kitchen, the Rev. William Greenlaw, "Hunger is getting worse." In fact, meals served have increased from 35 in 1982 to over 6 million in 2007.

During this time, homeless people, working-poor families, veterans, the mentally ill, a few addicts, and immigrants have lined up outside the Church from Monday through Friday. Inside, volunteers prepare lunch. Counseling and referral services have been available since 1986.

Holy Apostle Soup Kitchen is the largest in the United States. Soup kitchens can be found in many houses of worship nation wide, all trying to fill the human need for food and connectedness; and often medical, dental and psychiatric care, too.

What can you do to help end hunger and a lack of human connectedness? More than you know.

Come, you that are blessed by My Father...for I was hungry and you gave Me food...thirsty and you gave Me...drink...a stranger and you welcomed Me. (Matthew 25:34,35)

What can I do to end the scandal of hunger in our land, Jesus?

You Can Beat Burnout

If you're a so-called workaholic, you probably spend long, stressful hours either on the job or thinking about the job. But "all work and no play" isn't much of a life. It's a path to burnout.

Colleen Contreras, author and productivity specialist, offers five steps to beat burnout and balance your life:

- Remember, you are not alone. Reach out and regain perspective.
- Short-circuit the cycle. Stop what you're doing. Take a breath and a break. Go out for lunch or for a walk. Take a vacation.
- Be honest with yourself. Don't say 'yes' to additional commitments if you're already overwhelmed.
- Celebrate small wins. Appreciate even small accomplishments as well as the help of others along the way.
- Reset expectations. Set aside time for yourself every day.

Do not live to work. Instead, work to live.

Go, eat your bread with enjoyment, and drink your wine with a merry heart. (Ecclesiastes 9:7)

Carpenter from Nazareth, help us to put living and loving before work and career.

Simple Production, Profound Message

Before his death in 1999, stage actor Josef Meier never performed on Broadway, never won a Tony Award, and was not a "household name" recognized by many.

Yet, through his long-term commitment to community theatre, Meier had an instrumental part in breaking a record no Broadway production can claim.

For more than 60 years, Meier portrayed Jesus Christ in the famed Black Hills Passion Play. It is the longest-running professional passion play in the nation. Held in Spearfish, South Dakota, the play is described by observers as a marvel of outdoor pageantry and religious drama despite its somewhat simple imagery and staging.

You don't have to be famous or rich to make an impact on the lives of others. Pursue what you love, and blessings will likely flow from your efforts.

Remember what the Lord your God did. (Deuteronomy 7:18)

Steer me in the path of Your ways, Triune God.

Quick, Slow, Slow

QTH STS STA—mean anything to you?

These letters are a reminder that Archie Dunham, one time president of Conoco Oil Company, puts at the top of his notepad before meetings. They stand for "quick to hear, slow to speak and slow to anger" and come from the Epistle of St. James.

Dunham believes they help him use good judgment. "Learn to be a good listener; gather information from many sources; don't react too quickly to what you hear; and above all else, don't become angry," he says. "Anger impairs your ability to make good decisions. It also contributes to a poor attitude and can keep you from enjoying the many opportunities life has to offer."

Anger makes us prone to act emotionally rather than rationally. Taking the time to think things through and exercise our God-given reason can put problems in perspective.

Let everyone be quick to listen, slow to speak, slow to anger. (James 1:19)

Remind me to be as eager to hear others as I am to want them to hear me, Holy Wisdom. Show me how to balance reason and feelings.

Lend a Caring Heart

Being surrounded by loved ones may seem like the perfect way to leave this world, but for one dying woman all the flowers and jokes couldn't provide the real comfort she needed as she realized her life was coming to a close.

Then Margaret came along, and while her job was to clean the hospital floors at night, she made time to sit with the dying woman and listen to her.

She simply approached the woman and asked her if she wanted to talk about her suffering, since her family and friends preferred to avoid that topic. All Margaret could offer was someone who would listen, but it was all that was needed.

Follow her footsteps. Be a lover because love…

- is the most powerful way to reach out to someone
- trumps all material possessions.
- is the one thing all humans can offer each other.

Let us love, not in word or speech, but in truth and action. (1 John 3:18)

Give us the courage and stamina to love, Redeemer.

Save the Planet

With the threat of global warming looming over the earth, it's necessary now more than ever to make changes. Although some might not think it makes much of a difference, there are simple things each person can do to have an impact.

Switching to energy saving products and using less energy are two simple ways to contribute. So does using ground water to heat or cool your home.

Using public transportation, carpooling, or working closer to home would make a great difference especially if everyone started to do it.

Bring washable canvas bags to the store rather than using plastic or paper. At work, use the air conditioner, computer, and lights less to make a difference. Recycle paper not just the usual plastic, glass, and cans.

These are just some ways each person can help. What else can you do to help the planet?

Like good stewards of the manifold grace of God, serve one another with whatever gift each of you has received. (1 Peter 4:10)

Father, help us serve one another by our actions on behalf of the Earth, our common home.

Aging, Not Disengaging

When middle-aged Brad Edmondson noticed that his father Tom was sleeping more, leaving the house less and showing diminished concentration, he was concerned for himself as well as his septuagenarian dad. Were these inevitable signs of aging?

Edmondson thought so, until he attended a conference on aging. "I heard doctors and scientists agree that older people stay sharper when they stimulate their brains with lots of socializing and problem-solving."

The younger Edmonson introduced his father to a computer program meant to exercise the brain. He participated as well. In the process he helped his dad remain engaged with life. Too, they bonded. "We were talking more often, and he was telling me more about how he was feeling—which made me feel better," said Brad Edmonson.

Your family and your community need you. Become involved. Stay involved.

Those who honor their father atone for sins, and those who respect their mother are like those who lay up treasure. (Sirach 3:3-4)

Caring for elderly parents is not easy, God. Help us to be patient and tender with them and with ourselves.

The R.A.M. Expedition

Patients waited for hours in their trucks or in tents at Virginia's Wise County Fairgrounds. Then R.A.M. (Remote Area Medical) volunteer doctors, dentists, nurses, hygienists and X-ray techs arrived and flicked on their portable units, sterilized surgical instruments, and began seeing patients: 2,500 in 3 days. Others had to be turned away.

Nearly half live with at least one chronic condition—hypertension, arthritis, heart conditions, diabetes, major depression. Their teeth are rotten; dentures a must. Or they need glasses. Hospitals and primary-care physicians are in short supply for these and the other 47 million Americans who lack health insurance and medical care.

Dr. Scott Syverud says, "If you spend a day here, you see there's something wrong with health care in this country."

Do what you can to help.

Let the oppressed go free...share your bread with the hungry, and bring the homeless poor into your house...cover (the naked), and (do) not to hide yourself from your own kin. (Isaiah 58:6,7)

Guide our voting, letter writing and volunteering for our fellow citizens, Just Judge.

The Secrets of Being Happy

Are you happy? There's something you can do about it if you're not.

Here are some steps to achieving greater happiness from Noah Blumenthal, author of *You're Addicted to You: Why It's So Hard to Change—and What You Can Do About It.*

- Pretend every day is Thanksgiving. Find at least one thing for which you're grateful every day.
- Pat yourself on the back. What did you do well that gave you a sense of pride today?
- Plan a joyful activity. What will bring you happiness today?
- Spend time with someone who makes you smile.

Cultivate happiness, gratefulness, joyfulness. And do all you can to encourage others to do the same.

A joyful heart is life itself. (Sirach 30:22)

Beloved God, You know better than we do that it isn't easy to be joyful, cheerful, happy, grateful all of the time. So, help us.

What is Halloween?

Author and educator Anderson M. Rearick III knows that some Christians find Halloween spiritually harmful. He doesn't.

"I have always considered Halloween a day to celebrate the imagination," notes Rearick in *Catholic Digest*. "How delightful to go to parties with doughnuts, apples, brown cider, and pumpkin cakes—and to hear spine-tingling ghost stories." Rearick says Halloween allows "us to look at what frightens us, to experience it, to laugh at it, and to come through it."

On the Celtic New Year's Eve, *Samhain*, October 31, Celtic people extinguished their hearth fires, wore animal skin costumes, told fortunes and, after Druid priests predicted the future, relighted their hearth fires from a sacred bonfire.

By the 7th century, the Celts had become Christians. And *Samhain* had become *Alholowmesse*, a Middle English contraction of All Saints Day Eve, a celebration of God's faithful servants.

It's a good time to remind ourselves to truly be God's people—potential saints—in all we do.

Bless the Lord, spirits and souls of the righteous; sing praise to Him...forever. (Daniel 3:86)

Jesus, deliver us from fear of the imagination, fear of the unknown. Help us to trust You.

Always in God's Presence

God is everywhere. Yet we often act as though we don't really believe this truth. Perhaps that's why a book called *The Practice of the Presence of God* by Brother Lawrence of the Resurrection has been popular for 300 years.

Brother Lawrence was a French Carmelite lay brother and former soldier. With little education, he was assigned to menial tasks in his monastery and became known for both his holiness and his happiness. The book, published after his death, is a compilation of his letters and records made of his conversations.

Brother Lawrence stressed that we should remind ourselves of God's presence: "My most usual method is simple attentiveness and a loving gaze upon God, to whom I often feel united with more happiness and gratification than a baby at its mother's breast."

He also adds that "You need not cry very loud. God is nearer to us than we think."

O Lord, You have searched me and known me....Even before a word is on my tongue, O Lord you know it completely. (Psalm 139:1,4)

You are closer to me than my own heart, Merciful God. Moment by moment, help me to be aware of Your love.

Easing the Sting of Death

Writer Anne Raver offers a poignant account of her mother's death at age 94. She writes: "My mother, Kathleen Moore Raver, died so early in the morning that the sky was full of stars. She had been ready to go for a while, but her body wouldn't cooperate. 'I've lived a good life,' she kept saying. 'My bags are packed.' She had planned her own funeral years before, tucking a poem and other favorite writings into a packet.

"No eulogies," she ordered. "I want you to celebrate, dance and sing. Have a Scotch for me.'"

This is exactly what her children did as they recalled that she "was still pushing her walker past the barn to see what was blooming" even in her last days.

Because we are each irreplaceable, death's sting is severe. But comfort may be found in remembering a person's uniqueness.

"Where, O death, is your victory? Where, O death, is your sting?"...Thanks be to God, who gives us the victory through our Lord Jesus Christ. (1 Corinthians 15:55,57)

Comfort the grieving, Prince of Peace.

The Unlikely Spy

Helene Deschamps Adams was a teen during the Nazi occupation of her native France in World War II. Even at her young age, she hated it. In fact, she was so determined to help free her homeland that she joined the French Resistance.

Her youthful looks, charming demeanor and charming accent captured the attention and trust of German soldiers, enabling her to maintain her cover and be useful to the Resistance. Deschamps Adams reported the location of airfields and landmines. She witnessed the fatal shooting of a close friend who was also a spy and was herself nearly executed.

Years later, she characterized espionage as neither glamorous nor romantic, but a job that required one to "forget (one's) feelings."

Patriotism takes many forms. Voting is the most common exercise of citizenship, one that many take for granted. Exercise both your privilege and your right to vote in every election.

Render just decisions. (Deuteronomy 16:18)

Remind us, God, that governments derive their just powers from the consent of the governed.

No One's Beyond Redemption

The pastor of the Lockerbie, Indiana, United Methodist Church, the Rev. Chad Abbott, says his "church is a place of encouragement. We try to focus on what homeless people have to offer, not just their needs."

Several men living at a shelter joined the church's adult Bible study group. And because they described a system that didn't work, they "decided to get a few people together to see what they could do," says Mark Little who went on to be co-founder of a nonprofit called One Paycheck Away (OPA).

With the help of the church, OPA now prints and distributes a bimonthly newsletter geared to education and advocacy. A homeless carpenter built the coffee bar for the church's Earth House Coffee + Books which is mostly staffed by homeless or once homeless people.

Many homeless people are neither hopeless nor helpless. What can you do to encourage them?

Encourage one another and build up each other. (1 Thessalonians 5:11)

Abba, how can we not just encourage the homeless but ensure living wages and affordable housing for all?

Playbook for Life

"I'm the running back for the Seattle Seahawks football team," writes Shaun Alexander. "But it's not who I am."

A husband, father and man of faith, Alexander mentors youth from broken homes and shares lessons he learned growing up in similar circumstances. "Thankfully," he says, "I had a strong and wise Mom who was always there to show me love, to motivate me, to set me on the right path, to advise me."

Some notes from the Alexander playbook for life:

1. Be yourself.
2. Choose good role models.
3. Find the right words to live by.
4. Don't judge people till you've walked in their shoes. That helped him reconcile with his father.
5. Give. The Shaun Alexander Foundation is his way of showing gratitude "for the people God has put in my life."

What's in your playbook?

Offer to God a sacrifice of thanksgiving. (Psalm 50:14)

Jesus, as You were more than a Carpenter, so remind me to be more than my work.

Out of the Mouths of Babes

It wasn't even winter, yet the cafeteria at Van Meter Community School in Des Moines, Iowa was feeling a lot like Christmas. That's because the students, aged 11 to 14, had begun creating encouraging Christmas greetings for the students at an elementary school in Louisiana, many of whom had been made homeless by Hurricane Katrina.

Said fourth-grader and volunteer Tonisha Brookter, "My Christmas wish is to see all of the trailers gone in Louisiana, and all of the people there back in their homes."

The Van Meter School effort echoes what kids across the country have done to help others. According to one source, U.S. schoolchildren raised more than $10 million for Katrina relief.

Children deserve to be respected and protected. Yet, their only voice is that of caring, compassionate adults willing to speak out. Encourage legislation to guard children's rights.

Is there anyone among you who, if your child asks for a fish, will give a snake...for an egg, will give a scorpion? (Luke 11:11,12)

Merciful Savior, encourage all legislators and citizens to protect children and their rights.

A Green Vision

Van Jones has a vision: a cleaner, greener world where all of us collaborate in fighting pollution and poverty at the same time—a future for what might be called green-collar jobs.

Jones is an advocate for a solar panel enterprise in Oakland, California, and other projects that create jobs in environmentally aware construction and alternative energy. The Ivy League educated Jones is comfortable talking to inner city kids and Silicon Valley entrepreneurs and is good at uniting environmental activists and minorities.

The Oakland project uses unemployed workers to install solar panels which save home-owners money on energy. "Power by the people for the people," said Jones. "Polar bears, Priuses and Ph.D.s aren't going to do it alone. Everything our friends in the eco-elite do will vanish unless we find a way to expand green jobs to the rest of the economy."

Let's be creative in solving social and ecological issues.

By wisdom a house is built, and by understanding it is established. (Proverbs 24:3)

Holy Wisdom, guide our efforts to assure work for all and to undo environmental damage.

Modern Day Healers

According to recent statistics, 17 million Africans—including 2 million children—have died from AIDS. Another 25 million are infected with the HIV/AIDs virus. And 12 million African children have lost one or both parents to AIDS.

Brother and sister duo, Doctors Ellen and Bob Einterz use their passion, skills and dedication to relieve the devastation of the AIDS pandemic by providing "health care for some of the most desperate people of the world in sub-Saharan Africa."

From an early age, the doctors were raised to "live out their faith rather than wearing it on their sleeves." During their work, Drs. Ellen and Bob Einterz are reminded that they are "one small part of a greater world."

One person alone might not be able to change the world, but he or she can change at least one person's life. Each day use your God-given talents to show even one person God's faithful love.

Righteousness and justice are the foundation of Your throne; steadfast love and faithfulness go before You. (Psalm 89:14)

Compassionate Father, may I always exemplify Your faithful, compassionate love.

Need a "Happiness" Makeover?

These days, it sometimes seems that the mainstream media is obsessed with "making over" individuals; to radically change their outward appearance to gain greater happiness and satisfaction. But doesn't true happiness really come from within?

Happiness is often the result of an inner makeover, wherein a person actively chooses happiness over pessimism.

Consider these steps toward your own greater happiness:

- Itemize things big and small that make you happy. Pursue them.
- Schedule fun activities as you would obligations.
- Reserve time away from work, even if just a little each day.
- Take a deep breath, and list what's truly important. Don't let trivial things distract you.
- Revel in unplanned circumstances as opportunities, not setbacks.

Above all, place your hope and faith in God.

Happy are those who find wisdom, and... understanding. (Proverbs 3:13)

Guide me toward a more optimistic attitude, God.

Conquer with Kindness

As president during the Civil War, Abraham Lincoln carried the burden of millions of lives and the future of America. Yet he also showed concern for the fate of a single Confederate soldier.

Lincoln wrote to Union General William Rosencrans about a possible execution:

"I have examined personally all the papers in the Lyons case, and I cannot see that it is a matter for executive interference. So I turn it over to you with full confidence that you will do what is just and right; only begging you, my dear General, to do nothing in reprisal for the past—only what is necessary to ensure security for the future. I remind you that we are not fighting against a foreign foe, but our brothers, and that our aim is not to break their spirits but only to bring back their old allegiance. Conquer them with kindness—let that be our policy."

Show kindness to friend and enemy alike.

In passing judgment on another you condemn yourself...Do you not realize that God's kindness is meant to lead you to repentance? (Romans 2:1,4)

Help me show compassion for people I don't like or who don't like me, Just Judge.

Remembering Our Soldiers

Though he never served in the armed forces, Maine businessman Morrill Worcester does not want to forget those who gave their "last full measure of devotion."

Worcester, owner of a holiday wreath company, was moved by his first visit to Arlington National Cemetery when he was 12.

In 1992, when Worcester found he had a surplus of wreaths, he remembered Arlington. He secured permission and donated hand-made, hand-decorated wreaths. This effort is now called Wreaths Across America. Volunteers lay wreaths at military gravesites nationwide.

Tom Sherlock, Arlington Cemetery historian, says of the sea of stones, "if you...look at the name on the stone, in that moment, they're thought of again, and they live."

Let's honor those who have died for this country by working for peace with justice.

I know that my Redeemer lives, and that at the last He will stand upon the earth; and after my skin has been thus destroyed, then in my flesh I shall see God. (Job 19:25-26)

Help us to honor deceased members of the armed forces by working for that peace with justice for which they died, Prince of Peace.

Caring for Your Creativity

Each one of us has a spark of creativity within. But we each see that light in a unique time and place.

Martia Nelson already had a career when she first picked up a paintbrush in 1999. "I was so in love with painting, it felt like I was expressing my true self," she said in *Woman's Day* magazine. "I just wanted to share that, especially with people who would get such a tremendous benefit from it." She began to sell her work.

Nelson ultimately started a painting group for women with cancer. The women thrived in the supportive atmosphere where they could discover and express their creativity. Soon, Nelson's volunteer effort became a grant-funded activity.

"Every painting is like a love letter from the soul," says Nelson. "Your unconscious will get it, even if your conscious mind doesn't."

Nourish your creative gifts.

Like clay in the hand of the potter, to be molded as he pleases, so all are in the hand of their Maker, to be given whatever He decides. (Sirach 33:13)

Make me aware of the spark of creativity within me. Then, Jesus, help me fan that spark to bright flame.

A Police Dog's Best Friend

Back in 2000, when 10-year-old Stacey Hillman read an article about police dogs and their need for bulletproof vests, she thought that someone should do something about it—and she did.

The Florida native went to her local Police Department and then to the County Sheriff. Both gave the go-ahead for her to raise money. Next she made collection jugs out of bottles and put a picture of her with a police dog on them. She put these bottles in veterinarian's offices and in pet goods stores.

Her charity—Pennies to Protect Police Dogs—has raised more than $140,000 since it started, purchasing 180 bulletproof vests. Stacey Hillman promises to keep her cause going until every police dog in the whole country has a bulletproof vest.

Whatever cause we fight for deserves our best efforts, so that, in the end, our world will be a better place.

Be rich in good works. (1 Timothy 6:18)

We praise You, Lord, for You provide us with everything we need.

A Musician Who Cooks

For decades, Irving Joseph could be found in Broadway pits, doing gigs with singers at the Café Carlyle and the Algonquin, or playing Gershwin, Cole Porter, Richard Rodgers and Jerome Kern at the Oak Room of the Plaza, the Drake, the Biltmore, the Regency—really any joint in his beloved New York.

He played piano with the Tommy Dorsey Orchestra, then with an array of stars that included Lena Horne, Josephine Baker, Frank Sinatra, Patti LuPone, Rita Moreno and Shirley Bassey.

But this musician's romantic side extended beyond his playing and performances. Just ask his wife, Phyllis Dolgin. Every Valentine's Day until his death in 2000, Joseph would cook up a romantic feast for just the two of them. He even insisted that she stay away from their apartment while he cooked—and then come home and dress up for the occasion.

There's so much to each one of us—and we have so much to offer others.

Love, not in word or speech, but in truth and action. (1 John 3:18)

Composer of all life, I give You thanks this day for my many blessings.

A Small but Vibrant Congregation

Big things can come in small packages. For example, according to an article in *Church Life,* from the extent of their projects, you might not suspect that Christ Church in Geneva, Ohio, has an average Sunday attendance of only 37.

But the church has an active lay ministry with programs that assist teenage mothers, supply canned goods to a food pantry and operate a vacation Bible School to develop young leaders.

The parishioners find many ways to publicize their activities and make the most of what little they have. A parishioner who teaches at the local high school and runs the teen mother program also advocates for the girls and encourages them to complete their education. The goods donated to the pantry have labels attached that read "Need a hand? Call Christ Church" and include the parish's phone number and address.

That's an idea for every small congregation and every person—you can do more than you think.

I can do all things through Him who strengthens me. (Philippians 4:13)

Strengthen small parishes so that they can do great things for You and Your people, Lord.

A New Addiction?

"I don't have a problem," the South Korean teenager insisted. But his mother believed that he was addicted to compulsive computer use and sent him to the Internet Rescue Camp, a treatment program.

South Korea has been described as the world's most wired nation. That makes staying in touch with loved ones, having access to a vast store of information and simply having fun easier. But when overdone, it has negative consequences.

So South Korea is at the leading edge of combating computer compulsion. There are Internet-counseling centers where youngsters are monitored and kept busy with exercise and group activities.

"It is most important to provide them the experience of a life without the Internet," said a counselor.

It's up to adults to teach youngsters to use electronic media with moderation—and not as a substitute for interacting with other people and the world.

To get wisdom is to love oneself. (Proverbs 19:8)

Inspire youngsters to use computers, iPods, cell phones and other electronic media wisely, Paraclete.

Doctor Everything

He's treated music-artist Jimmy Buffett and news anchor John Chancellor. He's also seen many construction workers with sawed-off fingers, and commercial fishermen with chests crushed by winches.

Dr. Timothy Lepore is a surgeon, medical examiner, school physician, football team doctor, Lyme disease expert, and, since he moved to Nantucket island off the Massachusetts coast in 1983, the occasional Dr. Doolittle.

Compensation for his services is, at times, unconventional. Some people pay in lobsters, and one offered yard work for hernia surgery. From a South African restaurant worker unable to afford his appendectomy, he accepted a few oatmeal raisin cookies each week from the young man's place of business.

"He's everywhere; he does everything," says David Aguiar, a local police sergeant.

All of us play many roles in the course of a lifetime—or a day. The key is to approach every task with a loving heart.

Give the physician his place, for the Lord created him...they too pray to the Lord that He grant them success in diagnosis and in healing. (Sirach 38:12,14)

Open my heart to serve You, Healing Lord.

Fun Without Toys

NEWS FLASH! Children can have fun without high-tech toys, even without toys at all.

A newspaper story about possibly toxic toys was followed by some reassuring letters to the editor:

- "Think about safe, simple entertaining and perhaps even mildly educational playthings—books, balls, jump-ropes, arts and crafts supplies—that foster our children's imagination."

- "Here are my suggestions: 1. Organize trips to museums, zoos, parks, aquariums; 2. Take a walk and talk with your children; 3. Go to a local library's story hour. Check out books; 4. Sit quietly and read with your children; 5. Buy books for holidays and birthdays; 6. Volunteer with your child; 7. Attend family events at your house of worship; 8. Encourage children to join sports teams for activity and fun."

Parents, try a few of these suggestions soon.

Train children in the right way. (Proverbs 22:6)

Abba, remind parents to encourage their children's imaginations and intelligence.

Taxi Talk

Annie sat back in the taxi as it traveled to Indianapolis' airport. She had just finished a very successful meeting.

But now she was going home and, lately, the time she spent with her preteen daughter, was anything but smooth. During the ride, the driver shared his story—his growing up in Eritrea in Africa, and then fleeing his homeland because of war to come to America.

He spoke also of his three teens. "They face so many challenges and sometimes they're tough on my wife and me," he said. "But we all just love one another through it."

As Annie exited the taxi, she called home. Her daughter would just be getting home from school, and Annie had a three-word message for her, "I love you."

Sometimes we need to peel back the layers of life—the hurt and frustrations, especially—to find that core of love that sustains and strengthens us.

**Love one another deeply from the heart.
(1 Peter 1:22)**

Lord, strengthen me with Your love that I may face today's challenges with loving patience.

Sandwiches and Fleece Blankets — Free

When Vito Elia first came to the United States from Italy, he didn't have anything.

So now, around Thanksgiving, this Pelham Bay, Bronx, New York, deli owner gives away about 100 turkey sandwiches, each packed into a paper bag with potato chips and a soda. He hands out dozens of free fleece blankets and raffles off 30-pound turkeys as well—all free of charge.

"I know how it is," he says. "These seniors in this neighborhood don't have money, and I like to do anything I can to help."

Elia has also given out roses on Mother's Day and around Christmas invites Santa to entertain local kids.

"He's a good guy," says one neighborhood resident of this shop owner. "You don't find them like him."

If we take a good look around, we'll find a way to help others and express gratitude for what God's given us.

It is good to give thanks to the Lord, to sing praises to Your name, O Most High; to declare Your steadfast love in the morning, and Your faithfulness by night. (Psalm 92:1-2)

Steadfast Lover, let me be Your generous heart to the needy this day.

There's Nothing Merry About Debt

Holidays are a time of gift-giving, celebration and joy. Unfortunately, for some, holidays can also be a time of mounting debt and irresponsible spending.

Financial planning experts say that even one holiday season of overspending can have a long-lasting impact on your overall financial health. So, each time you're tempted to "shop 'til you drop," consider the following tips to keep your finances flourishing and your holidays happy.

- **Small can be special.** Consider a meaningful, well-chosen but modest gift rather than going for broke.

- **Personalize it.** If money's tight, give your time and attention. Send a loved one an invitation to spend quality time together.

- **Say—and send—something sweet.** A heartfelt message and a homemade sweet show that you care, without breaking your bank.

Remember, it's the heart, not possessions that make a day a holiday.

A new heart I will give you. (Ezekiel 36:26)

Holy Spirit, help me avoid the trap of materialism, substituting things for genuine feelings.

Listening and Caring

When was the last time you heard an elderly relative speak about his or her past? Were you annoyed? Delighted? Curious?

For elderly people, talking about their past "helps clear up minor depression, reverses feelings of isolation, and helps…boost physical and mental well-being," according to an article in *Spirituality and Health Magazine.*

Next time you visit an elderly relative:

- Look for an object—a book, knickknack, clothing, for example—to spark a conversation.
- Use scents because they bring back memories, even if your elderly relative cannot verbalize it.
- Make "reminiscing cards" using pictures from magazines or newspapers showing scenes from the past.
- Listen to unhappy memories; let the elderly person express sadness and doubts.

Kindness will never be forgotten.

**Kindness is like a garden of blessings.
(Sirach 40:17)**

It isn't always easy to be patient with relatives, Holy Spirit. Help me.

Memory Lane

How many times have you moved? How many times have you visited an old neighborhood?

For Kenji Jasper, to walk down memory lane in Fairfax Village, Washington, D.C., is to visit a place he no longer recognizes. Jasper says that the neighborhood used to have many disparities: for example, "you were just as likely to see a BMW as a broken-down van with a fender missing."

But now the neighborhood of his childhood is different. The gentrification of Fairfax Village has been monumental. Jasper notes that, "The neighborhood I remember is long gone, except in my mind, where it will live as long as I can remember it."

Revisit an old neighborhood. See how time has changed it—and remember, your old neighborhood lives in your heart.

Some...have left behind a name, so that others declare their praise. But of others there is no memory; they have perished as though they had never existed...they and their children after them. But these also were godly.
(Sirach 44:8-10)

Remind us, Ancient of Days, that those who forget the past are bound to repeat it.

Preparing a Thanksgiving Feast

Thanksgiving always brings images of cooking a huge feast and welcoming family members for a sit-down dinner. Thanksgiving is also a time to remember all the things for which we are thankful.

But for many people, having a big feast is not possible; nor do they have material things for which to be thankful. And so, people and churches go out of their way to welcome them.

Our Lady of Consolation Church in Vattman, Texas, hosts 1500 guests at its annual Thanksgiving dinner, auction and crafts fair. Catholic Charities of Camden, New Jersey, holds a multicultural holiday event. The students at New Hampshire's St. Anselm College help collect and give out hundreds of baskets to the needy. And St. Mark's Church in Vienna, Virginia, has a perfect antidote to holiday excess—its annual Thanksgiving clothing drive which involves volunteers from age 6 up.

How can you express your gratitude?

Father of orphans and protector of widows is God. ...God gives the desolate a home....He leads out the prisoners to prosperity, but the rebellious live in a parched land. (Psalm 68:5,6)

Generous Father, inspire me to express my thanksgiving through deeds of loving service.

Hope on the Run

Native Americans in the United States have a history marked by loss: losing land and language, even family, as well as confinement to reservations. They also have especially high rates of youth suicide and alcohol-related deaths.

But there's hope, particularly for young people. Wings of America gathers Native American youth from reservations across the country. Training them for national cross-country races, this non-profit organization provides the potential for healthier lifestyles, and opens doors to a better education and future.

And Wings teams deliver, with at least one member winning a boys or girls national title 20 times since the teams first attended a championship meet in 1988.

Solving a challenge in our lives can sometimes mean just running in the right direction.

Flee from sin as from a snake. (Sirach 21:2)

Stay by my side, Master. Guide my feet onto Your path of justice and peace.

A Word of Thanks

Why is a spirit of gratitude so hard to nurture? Why is it easier to complain than to appreciate all the gifts that God has given us?

More than 2,000 years ago, Cicero, the Roman statesman and orator said, "Gratitude is not only the greatest of virtues, but the parent of all the others." That's worth remembering as we go about our day-to-day lives—if we're not grateful, we cannot hope to grow spiritually.

Kent Crockett, writing in *Making Today Count for Eternity,* offered these thoughts:

- Thankfulness acknowledges that God is our provider.
- Thankfulness prevents a complaining spirit.
- Thankfulness creates a positive outlook on life.
- Thankfulness invites joy to dwell in our hearts.

Whatever pain and trials you endure, God is always there. Whatever joys and blessings you enjoy, God is always there. Take the time to say, "Thank You."

Offer to God a sacrifice of thanksgiving. (Psalm 50:14)

Blessed Trinity, You are always present, always loving. Thank You for Your gifts, for Yourself. Thank You.

Giving Angels

During the holiday season, many people find themselves in the giving mode, willing to help those less fortunate without asking for a reward in return.

The eighth graders of Brooklyn, New York's Lutheran Elementary School are a good example of having an open heart and being willing to give. All these students needed was the means to give, and when their principal, Lorraine Tuccillo, decided to give them money to help, these students became excited about giving.

An anonymous donor gave Tuccillo $2,500 for the students to give out. Each student came up with a unique way to help. For example, by buying diapers for teenage mothers, knitting mittens for children in another school, or sending gifts to soldiers in Iraq.

Do you have the courage to reach out to someone in need? Ask God for it, knowing that He'll support your good intentions.

Be rich in good works, generous.
(1 Timothy 6:18)

Inspire us, encourage us, to acts of generosity, Loving Lord.

Relieving Stress during the Holiday Season

Every holiday season is full of over-packed stores filled with people rushing to get the perfect gift. It's not unusual for most people to experience more stress during this time.

Here are some stress reducing tips from Dr. Jerry L. Harber:

Stop: Count to ten and say a prayer for patience.

Reflect: Try to identify the cause of your stress. Once you find the cause, say it out loud.

Analyze and Act: Step back from the problem. Look at it as though you're a third party. Find a solution.

Resolve: to talk to a friend, to make a list of priorities; or even, to just say no.

During the holidays and always, don't forget that God is always with you to help you find patience and joy.

I Myself will be the shepherd of My sheep, and I will make them lie down. ...I will seek the lost... bring back the strayed...bind up the injured, and...strengthen the weak. (Ezekiel 34:15,16)

Good Shepherd, bring us into Your sheepfold; keep us in Your sheepfold forever.

Awakening through Advent

In the weeks before Christmas, we sometimes neglect to think about what this holy day really means. That's what the season of Advent is for—and if we use it well, Advent can change us in ways we never imagined.

In *Seek That Which Is Above,* Cardinal Joseph Ratzinger, now Pope Benedict XVI, wrote: "Advent is concerned with that very connection between memory and hope which is so necessary to man. Advent's intention is to awaken the most profound and basic emotional memory within us, namely the memory of the God who became a child. This is a healing memory; it brings hope. The purpose of the Church's year is continually...to awaken the heart's memory so that it can discern the star of hope. ...

"It is the beautiful task of Advent to awaken in all of us memories of goodness and thus to open doors of hope."

Open your own door to hope.

A star shall come out of Jacob, and a scepter shall rise out of Israel. (Numbers 24:17)

Father, You bless us with Jesus, Your Son and our Savior. May we rejoice in His divine and human presence.

Log On and Pray

As our days fill up with yet one more item to add to our "to do" list, we may find our spiritual life a bit neglected—with even prayer time at a premium.

One office worker solved that dilemma by choosing for her computer passwords the names of people she wanted to remember in prayer. She even once chose the words "thank you" as her log on, and said a prayer of gratitude to God each day for her blessings.

Meanwhile, a salesperson offers silent prayers each day for patience to deal with difficult people. A businessman prays on his walk to work, remembering especially all who are ill. And during breakfast, two parents say a prayer for wisdom after getting the little ones ready for school.

In the whisper of a moment, we can reconnect with the Creator of all life, the source of all love.

My lips will praise You. So I will bless You as long as I live; I will lift up my hands and call on Your name. (Psalm 63:3-4)

Hear me, Lord, when I call for help. Help me bring Your love to others.

The Person Behind the Icon

A weary seamstress, Rosa Parks, refused to give up her bus seat to a white man one afternoon in 1955. In segregated Montgomery, Alabama, that was a crime.

Her arrest sparked a bus boycott led by the Rev. Dr. Martin Luther King, Jr., a key point in the growing civil rights movement. Later, Parks and her husband moved to Detroit, Michigan. After lawyer John Conyers was elected to Congress, she worked for him as an assistant. He said of her, "She was one of the most approachable heroes you could ever encounter."

Rosa Parks lived quietly until, in 1994, she was attacked and robbed in her home by a crack user. At the end of her life, she battled poor health. She died at age 92 in 2005.

A person's role in life sometimes eclipses their individuality. Think about your parents, spouse, children, employer, and neighbors. Remember that they, too, are people with unique feelings, hopes and dreams.

Do to others as you would have them do to you. (Luke 6:31)

May I see others through Your eyes, Jesus.

Remembering to Serve

It's easy to get caught up in routines. One man came to this realization after 25 years of volunteering as a soup kitchen pot washer at the University Parish of St. Joseph's in New York City's Greenwich Village.

Joe Caldwell was fed up with what he considered the carelessness and lack of common sense on the part of other volunteers: drains clogged with peelings and cuttings; dirty hands dipped into clean rinse water; casseroles welded to pans because they were not coated with cooking spray. Fed up, he was seriously thinking of quitting.

Then Caldwell remembered what was really important, why he and all the other volunteers were at this soup kitchen: to serve. He adds, "To *serve*. How wonderful the word! How inviting the act!"

When the little things grate, step back and remember what is really essential: serving God by serving others.

Serve one another with whatever gift each of you has received. (1 Peter 4:10)

Remind us of the dignity and nobility of loving service done in Your Name, Divine Master.

Keys to a Long Life

Your attitude toward life may affect your life span. According to a Yale University survey reported in *Prevention* magazine, "Being optimistic in middle age increases life span by at least 7.5 years—even after accounting for age, gender, socioeconomic status, and physical health."

Editors consulted longevity specialists and came up with these optimists' healthy habits

1. They work their phones: Just talking on the phone to a friend lowers blood pressure and cortisol levels.
2. They express gratitude. It's hard to be bitter or angry when you're feeling grateful.
3. They're randomly kind. One researcher found that five acts of kindness a day can boost your sense of well-being.
4. They reappraise their lives, viewing past unpleasant events as positive and motivating learning experiences.

Is your attitude helping you or hurting you?

What does the Lord require of you but to do justice, and to love kindness, and to walk humbly with your God? (Micah 6:8)

Help us make kindness to self, to others, to creatures our rule of life, God.

We Are Family

The Owensboro, Kentucky, women who meet weekly to make quilts form an extended family with the people who receive them, most of whom have AIDS. The quilters, part of the Catholic Diocesan Social Concerns Office, started their efforts in 1994.

By 2006 the women had pieced their 400th quilt and had decided to ask quilters from others churches to join them in quilting for hospice patients because "we're all alike and we all have the same problems."

They believe that AIDS "happens to the richest and the poorest...to people who go to church and people that don't...it happens to everyone...Whether you've had someone die of this dreaded disease or not...the fact is, we're all human beings, and we've got to help one another."

How true: We are human beings who can help one another.

When God created humankind He made them in the likeness of God. Male and female He created them, and He blessed them and named them "Humankind" when they were created. (Genesis 5:1-2)

How can I honor and support the humanity I share with those who have life-threatening diseases, Loving Father?

Christmas Outside the Box

"Mom, what I really want this Christmas is to spend more time with you," nine-year-old Elizabeth told her mother. Lately, the weekends for Ann and her daughter had been packed with activities that kept them doing things, but separately.

So Ann cleared their calendars. For the Saturdays in December, they would do things as a duo. There was a trip to the movies, afternoons of shopping, and time spent just sipping chocolate and eating cheese fondue at their favorite neighborhood restaurant.

As the month drew to a close, Elizabeth looked sad. "Don't worry," her mother reassured. "We'll keep living our Saturdays like this as often as we can all year." The little girl smiled, and her mom realized that her daughter's gift wish was hers as well.

Sometimes the gifts we give each other don't come in fancy paper. Often, they are found in an open heart and an abiding presence.

For everything there is a season, and a time for every matter under heaven. (Ecclesiastes 3:1)

Your gifts to us are many, Lord. Let us always find Your Presence in one another's presence.

Santa Claus Lives!

It's traditional for little children to line up to sit on Santa's lap at stores and malls and tell him what gifts they want for Christmas. Too soon they out-grow this and stop believing in Santa Claus.

So, the mission of the Amalgamated Order of Real Bearded Santas (A.O.R.B.S.) is to keep belief in Santa Claus alive for children and adults as a way of spreading Christmas cheer and faith. The founders of A.O.R.B.S. first met in 1994 after doing a commercial together. Since then the group has grown across the nation.

As for the real Santa Claus, he was St. Nicholas who lived in the late third century near Myra in present-day Turkey. He is said to have given away all of his inherited wealth and to have helped the poor and sick. He is the patron saint of children.

Embody him this Christmas for the child in you, in everyone. Play. Give gifts. But mostly share love.

Give good gifts to your children. (Luke 11:13)

Infant Redeemer, keep the child in me alive. Help me live, love, play, learn, and be childlike.

Body — and Soul — Food

Find your passion and help make the world a bit better. For Robin Miller of the Food Network's *Quick Fix Meals*, that passion is cooking and nutrition. But her path to discovery was painful.

Miller's beloved older sister had anorexia while in college. Although she had been both popular and gifted, and had a loving, close-knit family, she eventually died from the complications of the disease.

Miller wanted a positive way to remember her sister. So she chose to study nutrition and to encourage people to have a healthy relationship with food.

"At its best, at its deepest, food is a joy," writes Miller. "It's about sharing and nurturing. I put my heart and soul and passion into cooking for my family. I feel like I'm warming them from within and there is something spiritual about that."

Nurture others in any way you can.

Those who are cheerful and merry at table will benefit from their food. (Sirach 30:25)

Thank You, Lord of the Harvest, for the nutritious food and clean water with which You have blessed us.

The Strength of Mary

It would be a mistake to think of Mary of Nazareth as sheltered from ordinary life. Had she been, she could never be our exemplar of whole-souled living.

A faithful Jew, Mary lived in first century Roman-occupied Palestine within a patriarchal culture. Married at about 13, she went into labor and gave birth to her Son in a stable. As a wife and mother, Mary probably spent about 10 hours a day on domestic chores. As a middle-aged woman, she saw her beloved Jesus executed as a common criminal by the Roman army. The last time we glimpse her in the New Testament, she is with her Son's disciples at prayer.

Discovering Mary's real life makes her our model of faithfulness living amidst duties and obligations; cultural and political limitations. As her discipleship lay in listening to God and observing the Commandments, so does ours.

A capable wife('s)...husband trusts in her....She provides food for her household...considers a field and buys it...puts her hands to the distaff, and...spindle...reaches out...to the needy...makes linen garments and sells them...opens her mouth with wisdom and...kindness.
(Proverbs 31:10,11,15,16,19,20,24,26)

Jesus, remind me of Your mother's discipleship.

A Natural-Born Fundraiser

Diana Campoamor was just 6-years-old when she embarked on her first fundraising effort. It was 1955. She and her family had just returned to their home in Havana from their farm, and the girl wrote her Christmas gift list. "The children of the campesinos I had played with were poor so I made a list of bequests for them, too," she recalls.

When Campoamor received her Christmas presents, she was haunted by her parents' admission that the *campesinos'* children did not get any. "It wasn't fair that they couldn't have things that I could," she says.

This event marked the start of a life of giving. Campoamor went on to head Hispanics in Philanthropy (HIP), one of the world's largest non-profit organizations dedicated to raising money for needy Latinos in North and South America.

The innocence of children often allows them to see reality more clearly than we adults do.

(Jesus) said, "Truly I tell you, unless you change and become like children, you will never enter the kingdom of heaven." (Matthew 18:2-3)

Help us to see with a child's eyes; to believe with a child's soul, Abba.

Beat Stress During the Holidays

Many people find holidays stressful. They cost time, energy and money and can cause conflicts between family members and friends. They can also be depressing times for people without close loved ones, or those who have lost loved ones, or who feel over burdened or lonely.

The *Wyoming Catholic Register* suggests these remedies:

- Avoid spending too much money by making homemade gifts.
- Create new holiday traditions to fit changed circumstances.
- Don't let differences between family members or friends get in the way of the holiday spirit of good will.
- When feeling alone, turn to another. No one should be alone.

This season, plan ahead for the stress or loneliness that lies ahead. And try to enjoy the holiday in your way.

Rejoice in the Lord always; again I will say, Rejoice. (Philippians 4:4)

At holiday times, Lord Christ, soothe us when we are stressed; let us know the embrace of Your consoling arms.

The Joy of Giving

Christmas, Hanukkah and Kwanza can be sad, lonely and disappointing for the children of prison inmates and ex-inmates.

So restaurateur Carol Redding and *New York Daily News* court reporter Chrisena Coleman teamed with In Arms Reach, a community not-for-profit for children whose parents are or were in jail.

Redding and Coleman have collected thousands of books, items of clothing and toys. They wrap the gifts and make surprise deliveries to the children and their families.

Redding promises to again "play Santa on Christmas Eve" this year. And Coleman says, "Delivering toys to children will bring our vision of spreading holiday cheer full circle."

In Arms Reach Executive Director Terrence Stenens adds, "Many of the children have no Christmas at all. The gifts will help fill a void in their life."

These folks bring holiday cheer to needy children. How can you do the same?

Blessed are the merciful, for they will receive mercy. (Matthew 5:7)

Gentle Jesus, how may I bring cheer to children and the lonely, elderly or sick at this time when we celebrate Your birthday?

Celebrate the Lady of Guadalupe

Each December 12, Mexican and Mexican-American Catholics celebrate the 1531 appearance of *La Virgen Morena,* the virgin of Guadalupe, to the Aztec Juan Diego near Mexico City.

For example, at Tortugas Pueblo, Las Cruces, New Mexico, the Corporacion de los Indigenas de Nuestra Señora de Guadalupe has a three day celebration. On December 10, there is a candlelit procession, a novena and dancing by the group *Danzantes.* The next day, there's a pilgrimage to the summit of the Tortugas Mountain for confession, another novena and the lighting of a mountaintop cross. And on the 12th, there is a liturgy and dancing afterwards. The day ends with food, a rosary and a procession.

Our Lady of Guadalupe is called the patron and mother of the Americas. All of us can imitate her faith-filled discipleship and love of God's children.

You shall love the Lord your God with all your heart, and with all your soul, and with all your mind, and with all your strength. ...Love your neighbor as yourself. (Mark 12:30,31)

Son of God, help us to imitate Your Mother.

Ever Green Christmas

A Christmas tree is an essential part of the Christmas season for many of us. We decorate it, put gifts under it and celebrate around it. However, a tree is much more than a beautiful tradition.

In December, 2004, Pope John Paul II said: "The traditional Christmas tree is a very ancient custom which exalts the value of life, as in winter the evergreen becomes a sign of undying life. …It reminds us of 'the tree of life' (Genesis 2:9) and is a representation of Christ, God's supreme gift to humanity.

"The message of the Christmas tree, therefore, is that life is 'ever green' if one gives: not so much material things, but of oneself—in friendship and sincere affection, and fraternal help and forgiveness, in shared time and reciprocal listening."

This Christmas let the ever green spirit of hope and goodness dwell in your heart and, in turn, bless all you meet.

**Greet one another with a holy kiss.
(1 Corinthians 16:20)**

Infant of Bethlehem, may the love that sent You among us bless us all of our days.

Soup Kitchen Stories

"The more we give away. The more we get," said Vincent Smith, parish manager at St. John's Roman Catholic Church in Newark, New Jersey, about the huge sack of potatoes a donor had left. Volunteers serve thousands of meals to guests like these:

Thirty-something Charles says that he "was good...until seventh grade. Then my whole world just crumbled. I couldn't really control it."

Middle-aged Carolyn, who misses the time she felt useful to her family, has a serious illness. Speaking of her family she says, "They don't need you no more. When you come over, they can't wait for you to leave."

Leon, another soup kitchen guest, hungers to see his teenaged daughter "before it's too late or before she's grown."

Guests at soup kitchens and shelters hunger for family and human connection as much as they hunger for food.

Be doers of the word, and not merely hearers. (James 1:22)

Inspire volunteers at shelters and soup kitchens to reach out to their guests with genuine affection, Spirit of Love.

Grief in a Time of Joy

There's never an easy time to mourn the loss of a loved one, but the holidays can be especially difficult.

Journey, the newsletter of the National Catholic Ministry to the Bereaved, offers suggestions for caring for yourself even as you grieve for another at Christmastime. Here are some ideas:

- Start a new tradition with a special gift to a charity in your loved one's name.
- Invite someone who would otherwise spend the holidays alone to join your celebration.
- Rearrange the seating around the dinner table.
- Open gifts at a different time.
- Decorate your home in a new way.
- Spend time with family and friends.

Give yourself permission to enjoy yourself. It may be hard to celebrate when you miss someone, but try to relax and have some fun. That does not mean you love that person any less.

Be comforted for your grief. For grief may result in death, and a sorrowful heart saps one's strength. (Sirach 38:17-18)

Paraclete, my Comforter, help me to trust You to console me in hard times.

Paper or Plastic?

As a nation, we use 380 billion plastic shopping bags each year and recycle only an estimated 5.2 percent. The rest end up in landfills where they don't decompose and pose a hazard to wildlife, or clog pipes and drains.

Not only that, but the manufacture of plastic shopping bags consumes 1.6 billion gallons of oil each year.

Some cities are taking action. San Francisco has begun an effort to promote bags that can be composted, while encouraging financial support for cleanup and recycling from food retailers with sales over $2 million a year and drugstores with more than 5 locations. Other cities are considering similar measures.

But why wait? Encourage local vendors to use paper sacks. Even better, choose sturdy, attractive canvas sacks for purchases which can be laundered and repaired. And when worn out, canvas decomposes easily. See, you *can* easily make a difference.

The Lord, who created the heavens...formed the earth and made it (He established it; He did not create it a chaos, He formed it to be inhabited!) (Isaiah 45:18)

Refresh our reverence for Your Earth which we call home, Eternal Creator.

At Christmas, Less Really is More

Terri Cettina recalls when she and her husband, Greg, both worked corporate jobs. "We were swept up in the pursuit of perfectly selected and wrapped Christmas presents," she admits.

Then Greg lost his job while Terri was working part-time to care for their new baby. They "decided not to give up our traditions," she says. Instead, they wisely cut back Christmas activities.

- First, they earmarked a specific dollar-amount to spend on gifts and kept to that limit.
- Next, by choosing gifts more carefully, they avoided lofty price tags.
- Finally, to end last-minute impulse-buying, the couple shopped earlier in the season.

As a result, the Cettinas focused on the real meaning of Christmas and not on the material.

How can you help remind yourself and others that Christmas is more than a retail event?

God's love has been poured into our hearts through the Holy Spirit that has been given to us. (Romans 5:5)

In giving us His only begotten Son, the God of Israel bestowed the Gift of gifts on His world.

Quiet, Quick and Accomplished

Quiet and quick describes Oklahoman Angel Goodrich, a 5-foot-3 basketball player who was one of the reasons her Sequoyah High School team in Tahlequah, Oklahoma, made it to the top 10 in a *Sports Illustrated* national poll.

She is the first Division I athletic scholarship recipient in school history. Goodrich's accomplishments would have been incomprehensible to earlier generations at the school. Located in the Cherokee Nation, it was established in 1871 as an Indian orphanage and later an institution for the so-called incorrigible. These days it has good facilities and high standards.

Although Goodrich is a trailblazer, it hasn't gone to her head. Her coach Bill Nobles keeps things in perspective. "My first goal isn't to win ballgames, it's for them to have a successful life," he says. He also preaches, "No alcohol or drugs. Do not fear failure."

Do your best—and never fear failure.

Fear is nothing but a giving up of the helps that come from reason.
(Wisdom of Solomon 17:12)

Lord, help us find our inner reserves of bravery.

Reasons for Hope

The urge to despair at our troubled world is understandable. Yet everyday brings reasons to hope. For example, writing in *Newsweek* magazine Mary Carmichael highlights a doctor, a banker, an engineer and a scientist with a "doggedly optimistic attitude" in their search for an HIV/AIDS vaccine.

Dr. Fred Binko, executive director of INDEPTH, is overseeing the creation of a Ghanaian database recording births, deaths, marriages and medical histories. This information is a prerequisite for clinical trials. Christopher Egerton-Warburton, an Oxford trained financier, works to "transform immunization into an investment opportunity" attracting wealthy donors.

Engineer David Edwards believes that in time patients will be able to ward off disease with a cheap inhalable powder. Biologist Emilio Emini is searching for an AIDS vaccine.

Whether it's a disease or a problem, there are always reasons for hope. Cling to hope!

Hope does not disappoint us. (Romans 5:5)

Imbue me with hopefulness and with faith, Holy Spirit.

Extra! Extra! Read All About Christmas!

Lee Strobel felt called to track down hard answers to the great questions of the Christian faith.

The exploration led this legal affairs editor for the *Chicago Tribune* to become a Christian—and to examine the facts surrounding Christmas.

In his book, *The Case for Christmas,* Strobel concludes that the Gospel writers are, in fact, dependable reporters of true, factual events—and not the spinners of religious myth. From the census to King Herod to the Star of Bethlehem, this author reveals how much we really do know—for a fact—about that life-changing event in human history, the birth of Jesus.

"By the standards of ancient history, the Gospels are a veritable news flash," Strobel notes.

The reality of God's presence in our world as found in the loving witness of believers is another perennial truth. How can you witness to God's moment-by-moment presence?

You will be My witnesses...to the ends of the earth. (Acts 1:8)

Live in my mind and my heart today, Blessed Trinity, that I may witness Your healing loving presence.

A Cat After Catastrophe

Arlene Badalementi saw a story in her local newspaper—and then couldn't say no.

"I saw that cat's little face and couldn't resist," she said about the photo that accompanied the tale of an abused cat. "My heart just went out to him."

The family immediately adopted the stray cat that had been badly beaten and thrown off a six-story building. The vicious attack left the animal—whom the Badalementis named Mickey—with multiple injuries.

These days, Mickey is safe and hanging out with this caring family's two other cats and their dog. "They all get along; he fits right in with the crew," says Joseph Badalementi.

"Everyone who pitched in to save his life should get kudos for that," says Arlene.

Accomplishing good things takes the goodwill of all. Who or what needs attention in your neighborhood?

Whenever we have an opportunity, let us work for the good of all. (Galatians 6:10)

Guide me where You need me, Lord. Help me bring Your love into my every day; to all the people and creatures I meet.

Showcasing the Christmas Spirit

During the Christmas season, many people walk through the streets of large cities like New York to gaze at department stores' holiday-themed windows. But do you know about the companies that creates these displays?

David Spaeth, owner of Spaeth Designs, creates such holiday treatments. One year, Spaeth found a glitch, one that could have ruined one store's display. The elaborate Nutcracker design he created operated with one switch. The night before the display was to be sent to the store, the scene was not working.

Spaeth turned to God in his moment of need. "God, I don't know what to do...Please help," said Spaeth. The answer came to him in using different switches for each segment of the display. The display was recreated and was a hit with customers.

In a moment where time is against you, always remember that God is with you.

Abide in Me as I abide in You. (John 15:4)

Sweetest Savior, remind me to nestle in Your everlasting arms, close to Your loving heart.

Getting the Mail Through...

We've all heard the saying "the mail must go through." But there are times when it takes a lot longer than others.

On December 23, 1914, a postcard with a colored drawing of Santa Claus was sent to Ethel Martin of Oberlin, Kansas, from cousins in Alma, Nebraska. It never arrived—until the Christmas season of 2007. Ethel Martin had died, but the post office tracked down relatives and delivered it to her sister-in-law Bernice Martin. The card was inside another envelope with current postage.

"We don't know much about it," Bernice Martin said. "But wherever they kept it, it was in perfect shape."

That mystery may never be solved, but it's good to know that at the end someone took responsibility for seeing that a 93-year-old greeting made it through.

Each of us needs to accept personal responsibility for our work and for the way we treat friend and stranger alike.

Owe no one anything, except to love one another; for the one who loves another has fulfilled the Law. (Romans 13:8)

Guide my efforts, Eternal Father, to serve Your people with respect for love of You.

The Right Choice

Every parent is a teacher. Howard Stier, writing in *Bits & Pieces,* recounts what his father taught him.

Stier's father, a Polish immigrant, had a little grocery store in a Pennsylvania coal-mining town. On Christmas Eve in 1943, the man discovered an extra $20 in the till and figured out the customer to whom it belonged. Even though there was a snowstorm, the two Stiers walked half an hour to return the money to its grateful owner.

A few months later, the man left town without paying his outstanding bill to the grocer. When the boy reminded his dad about the Christmas Eve incident, the man said, "We all have choices. It was my choice to do what I felt was right. His choice was not to pay his bill."

We all have choices. Deciding to do what's right rather than what's easy may cost us something, but never as much as doing what's wrong.

If you choose, you can keep the commandments, and to act faithfully is a matter of your own choice. (Sirach 15:15)

Spirit of Wisdom, guide me in making good and wise choices, not only for my own sake, but for others as well.

What We Keep and What We Give

We sometimes speak of observing or keeping holidays, but writer Linda Felver has a different take on that idea. In *A Book of Christmas*, she says:

"Let me not wrap, stack, box, bag, tie, bundle, seal, KEEP Christmas.

"Christmas kept is liable to mold.

"Let me give Christmas away, unwrapped, by exuberant armfuls. Let me share, dance, LIVE Christmas unpretentiously, merrily, responsibly with overflowing hands, tireless steps and sparkling eyes.

"Christmas given away will stay fresh—even until it comes again."

This year, try giving away your Christmas—with love—not only to those near and dear to you, but also to those who might not otherwise experience the joy of Jesus' birth.

A child has been born for us, a son given to us;...He is named Wonderful Counselor, Mighty God, Everlasting Father, Prince of Peace. (Isaiah 9:6)

Son of God, show me how to welcome You by welcoming Your children into my life each day of the year.

Doctors on Wheels

For many families in the United States, paying for doctor visits is a hardship. In fact, nearly nine million kids lack health insurance. And 75 percent of uninsured children have at least one parent who works full time, but cannot afford private insurance.

But there's hope—and it may be pulling up and parking in your neighborhood.

The Children's Health Fund (CHF) supports a national network of programs that bring medical services to kids who need care. CHF works with hospitals or health clinics, and even sends medical vans to make weekly visits to schools, homeless shelters and other neighborhood sites.

"That's the fun thing about being mobile," offers Dr. Heidi Sinclair who heads a CHF children's outreach project in Baton Rouge. "You can go where the need is."

Each day we should search out the people in our lives who need help and healing.

Do not neglect to do good and to share what you have, for such sacrifices are pleasing to God. (Hebrews 13:16)

Divine Master, send Your Spirit to refresh and heal us.

Woodcarving for a Higher Purpose

Konstantinos Pylarinos does not have to "market" his skills or his creations. In fact, Pylarinos has more admirers of his work than he knows what to do with.

From his Astoria, New York, workshop, the Byzantine-style woodcarver makes furniture for Greek Orthodox churches. He makes bishop's thrones, baptismal fonts and icon frames. But his specialty is the iconostasis, the large panel of icons separating the sanctuary from the congregation. His work is admired by many; some even thank God for the chance to see his carvings.

The iconostasis he carved for an Ontario church is made up of 56 separate, interlocking pieces which requires complicated assembly and spans over 50 feet in width and 15 feet in height.

Born of his childhood admiration for the exquisite churches of his native Greece, Pylarinos' work is in churches around the globe. What a unique way to bring God into the lives of others!

How are you showing God to others?

(The Lord) filled him with divine spirit, with skill, intelligence, and knowledge in...carving wood. (Exodus 35:31,33)

Abide with us in our journey, Lord Christ.

Going Green At the Office

Do you remember the words of Kermit the Frog, "It's not easy being green..."?

Apparently, corporate America remembers Kermit's lament even as "going green" is getting easier and easier, thanks to the efforts of architects such as Robert Fox, Jr. and Richard Cook.

The architects' own office received New York's only platinum rating from the United States Green Building Council, a non-profit group that sets and recognizes adherence to guidelines known as LEED—Leadership in Energy and Environmental Design. LEED encourages building owners to conserve energy and water, among other environmentally friendly goals.

The architects say that they "believe in creating the right kind of environment" with plenty of natural light, energy-saving appliances and even a place to compost waste.

Good business and environmental concerns need not be mutually exclusive. Respect your environment every where, every day.

I made the earth, and created humankind upon it. (Isaiah 45:12)

Blessed be all of Your creations, Spirit of God.

Celebrating 100 Years

Lawrence Lucie may not sport the same snazzy suits and hairstyle that he did in 1934, when he played with Benny Carter at Harlem's Apollo Theater. Nor is he as spry and energetic as when he played the Cotton Club with Duke Ellington.

But when he celebrated his 100th birthday in 2007, he still had an uncanny ability to hold people in thrall.

Fans and musicians alike gathered to honor the jazz musician who was a behind-the-scenes legend, since he did not share the level of fame that some of his co-performers attained. However, his critical acclaim remains steadfast, as members of the jazz community recognize the contribution Lucie made to music.

Says one admirer and university jazz-studies director, "He is like a whole living history of jazz...he has played on so many important records."

Whatever you do, do it to the best of your ability.

Hold fast to the Lord your God. (Joshua 23:8)

Remind us to do our work to the best of our ability, Jesus, regardless of external recognition.

Thrifty Neighborliness

Jesus said that "whoever has two coats must share…and whoever has food must do likewise." (Luke 3:11) But how share without straining one's own budget? Here are some suggestions.

Elderly and infirm neighbors and new parents could use your help with minor home repairs, heavy house and yard work, the laundry, snow removal and more. Give a caregiver time away. Baby-sit for new parents. Ease isolation with the gift of your presence over tea or coffee.

For neighbors who aren't that near, those unused cans of food, for example, could help a soup kitchen's meal-planning. Or those unused cosmetics, toiletries, clothes, especially business clothes, and small appliances could help people get back on their feet, secure a job and furnish an apartment.

Think, who needs you to be their neighbor?

Give, and it will be given to you…for the measure you give will be the measure you get back. (Luke 6:38)

Merciful Savior, who is my neighbor?

The Value of Our Days

Michael Josephson wrote a reflection, "What Will Matter." According to him, the value of each one of our days will be measured by:

- What we built
- What we gave
- What we taught
- Our character
- Every act of integrity, compassion, courage or sacrifice that enriched, empowered or encouraged others to emulate us
- The memories that live in those who loved us
- How many will feel a lasting loss when we're gone
- How long we will be remembered by whom and for what

Josephson goes on to say that "living a life that matters" is a "matter of...choice."

Today, now, choose to live a life that matters.

The days of our life are seventy years, or perhaps eighty, if we are strong...teach us to count our days that we may gain a wise heart. (Psalm 90:10,12)

Holy Wisdom, help me to live a life that matters.

Also Available

Have you enjoyed volume 43 of *Three Minutes a Day*? These other Christopher offerings may interest you:

- **News Notes** – published 10 times a year on a variety of topics of current interest. Single copies are free; quantity orders available.

- **Ecos Cristóforos** – Spanish translations of select News Notes. Issued 6 times a year. Single copies are free; quantity orders available.

- **Wall or Desk Appointment Calendar** – The Calendar offers an inspirational message for each day.

- **DVDs/Videocassettes** – Christopher videos range from wholesome entertainment to serious discussions of family life and current social and spiritual issues.

For more information on The Christophers or to receive **News Notes, Ecos Cristóforos** or a catalogue:

The Christophers
5 Hanover Square
11th Floor
New York, NY 10004
Phone: 212-759-4050 / 888-298-4050
E-mail: mail@christophers.org
Website: www.christophers.org

The Christophers is a non-profit media organization founded in 1945. We share the message of personal responsibility and service to God and humanity with people of all faiths and no particular faith. Gifts are welcome and tax-deductible. Our legal title for wills is The Christophers, Inc.